Who Turned Off the Lights?

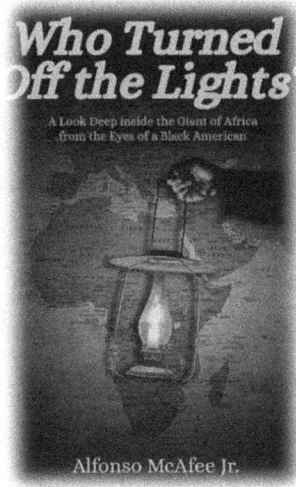

A look deep inside the GIANT of Africa from the eyes of a Black American?

By Al McAfee

Who Turned out the Lights?

COPYRIGHT PAGE

© 2020 by Al McAfee

You can contact me for copies and other pertinent concerns at:
mcafeedesign2014@outlook.com

Cover by Butterfly Graphix

ISBN: 978-1-7361891-0-8

Who Turned out the Lights?

PROLOGUE

Who turned off the light? The land before the country called Nigeria came into existence, was a land filled with light and hope. Electricity referred to as "light" metaphorically represents the success of the people. Today, lights are sporadic at best, and hope fading. Some believed darkness resulted from the colonization by the British, which brought about the ideals of capitalism. The survival of the fittest became the contest of the day and poverty surly followed. After Nigeria received its independence in 1960, the British left a system in place where the Northern region welded control over the Southern and Western regions. Many leaders felt the only way to change this system was through force. The first military coup was initiated by Igbo army officers in January 1966, this set off a series of counter coups including a bloody three (3) year civil war until the final coup d' etat in 1993. The untimely death of the Military head of State Sani Abacha paved the way for a civilian government.

As military rule became a seemingly permanent feature of Nigerian politics. Many Nigerians lost hope and developed a mindset to get all; as much as you can today, because tomorrow is just another day. Many civil servants took on the attitude of the increasingly authoritarian and corrupt governments. Greed, bribery, and corruption was the order of the day, over time corruption would reach almost every sector of life, and business dealings in the country. As a result of the "winner take all" framework, long regaining leaders referred to as strongmen dominated politics in Africa.

Nigeria provides power/electricity to the Ghanaian people that reside in Ghana, West Africa. Currently the energy supply crisis in Nigeria refers to the ongoing failure to provide adequate electricity supply to domestic households and industrial producers, only 40% of the Nigerian population is connected to the energy grid. It is so common in people residing in local communities, and villagers often state "we have a generator so that makes our family better than yours". The Federal Government of Nigeria spent Billions of dollars on roads, yet the country has some of the worst roads in the world. The Federal Government has also spent billions on the construction of Power Plants to bring stable lights to the country. Greed and corruption for roads, power facilities, and other necessary infrastructure projects have been squandered by corrupt leaders.

Anyone called to bring the thieves' to order are also bribed. It is often rumored that personal generator sales are so lucrative (Nigerians spend an estimated $14 Billion a year to buy and run them) to a select few would stifle the development of a steady power supply at the expense of its people, and development of the country.

Who Turned out the Lights?

The book is titled *"Who Turned off The Lights"* because of it duel request to turn on the physical light via fighting corruption, and the mental light by a change in the community mind set. Revolution is needed but the revolution may not be televised, nor may it be a radical or violent act.

I would like to make it abundantly clear that I am not advocating, nor calling for violence. The revolution must take place in the minds of more citizens, beginning to understand that through continuous access to technology steady lights are a necessary part of a developing country. Many Nigerians hate corruption, and greed with a passion, but feel powerless to do anything about it.

Access to the internet has brought about a new awareness of the power, and unity is empowering and enlightening the minds of the citizenry, especially the youth (with a population of over 210 million 50% under the age of 30). When more citizens realize that it is ok to demand their leaders to provide electrical power, and good roads, and that peaceful protest in the words of former US Congressman John Lewis is "good trouble". We therefore pray that love for country is more than lip service, but a sacrifice that many Nigerian must live for, and even perhaps willing to die for.

Who Turned out the Lights?

If a man has not found something in life he is willing to die for he is not fit to live.

  - **Dr. Martin Luther King, Jr.**

Darkness cannot drive out darkness; only light can do that. Hate cannot drive out hate; only love can do that.

  - **Martin Luther King Jr.**

Who Turned out the Lights?

Contents

<u>DEDICATION</u>

"Who Turned Off The Lights" is dedicated to my beloved brother Adrian A. McAfee who proved, the strength of two working together is an undeniable blessing, now as one, I promise to insure that his service to humanity will be remembered.

PREFACE

WHO turned *off* the LIGHTS?

A look deep inside the Giant of Africa from the eyes of a black American

I often ask myself, am I the only author in a world of over 7.7 Billion people who question what is my purpose for being here on this earth? How did human existence come about? Why can't I have immorality and would I even want to never die? When these questions come to mind, it's only through will power and strength of the spirit that I am able to shake off the troubling thoughts that cause long-term anguish.

As a risk taking business leader, my travels brought me to the continent of Africa. I did not go to the continent under the influence of a Multinational Corporation, a financial donor nor with any political or humanitarian curiosity. After the completion of three projects, I wondered could our Black American Construction firm be the first to return to the Motherland (African Continent) and find success, since the great slave trade commencing in the 15th century. Perhaps not, but my hope and prayers are that we certainly won't be the last.

Who Turned out the Lights?

After the loss of my beloved brothers, Uncle and two of the firm's most experienced and loyal field supervisions, I became quietly depressed. Due to my search for internal comfort, along with questions I had regarding my own mortality, I began writing this book *"who turned off the lights"*. It is through this spiritually guided endeavor that I may have found a source for hope and healing, not only for myself, but for a Nation and Continent as well.

INTRODUCTION

As a child in a family of ten with eight brothers and one younger sister, me being the sixth child, we were a very physical group. My older siblings would often use force during play. I recall being pinned to the ground and held there until I responded in a state of unnatural anger. At that point my siblings would become frightened, release me, and run. They never knew my raucous temperament was a well-crafted maneuver utilized to insure my freedom. If they knew my inner disposition my brothers would've been surprised, because they would've discovered that the entire escapade was simply a mental trick.

Chapter One, "**The Sun**" and Chapter Two, "**Three 40 Five**" serve as an educational bedtime story for parents with children. The initial chapters could be considered a biography of the author from childhood to adolescence. The author traces early life's steps describing a loved and protected child, which reached normal maturity level despite tragedies occurring around him. Additionally, it was through love and community guidance that he became revered and honored. A few sayings relative to the author are, "More is expected from those abundantly blessed", "The creator placed a fork in the road", and "Discover what direction the author chose to take."

Chapter Three, **"Africa"**, is the author's humorous and informative section. Once the first page of the chapter is viewed, although you will not see an indecent image, your first mind will surely say "wow that is big". The author presents a variety of facts thought to be important for the reader to know about the African Continent, and Nigeria in particular. The author provides information and data that you may not have known. Chapter Three is written to broaden your knowledge and remove some of the negative propaganda cast upon the continent by the world press.

Chapter Four, **"The Giant of Africa"**, invites the reader to imagine going on a journey with the author back through time. You may sense the shock of someone who appears to have departed a kinder, more gentle place, only to return to find things alarmingly displeasing and different. During travel throughout the land, the authors described some of the customs, traditions and beliefs that make Nigerian's unique. Chapter four also takes a bite into "the giant's" swagger. Although the bite may seem deep, the author's intention is not to draw blood, but to increase knowledge with respect to heritage and perception.

Chapter Five, **"The Courage to Hope"**, describes the conditions, struggles, and challenges of a people living in a country with unimaginable potential, and an abundant wealth of natural resources. In light of the riches, why are so many Nigerian's suffering? The author also highlights positive changes and the potential for a promising future.

Chapter Six, **"Chocolate City",** is intended to be of interest to Black Americans and other minorities. Based on statistical data, the American system of justice and its institutions are considered unjust and indifferent. Using Nigerian lingo *"with all things being equal"*, the author places a Black American in a typical night time police traffic stop. However, in this case, the Black American was not in Baltimore, Maryland, but in the African "Motherland" where the institution of discrimination should not exist against blacks. As you continue reading you will discover how this true life scenario is played out in a real chocolate city.

Chapter Seven, **"The Ancient City of Benin",** explains how, prior to 1957, Europeans colonized almost one hundred percent of the world's second largest continent. Chapter Seven outlines a case study that details how political control was established in a distinctive nefarious way. It will be interesting to know who and how insensitive the conquering fighting men were when it came to having mercy on older people, women and children during the "Benin Punitive Expedition".

Chapter Eight, **"Dubious Distinction"**, details circumstances that led to confidence tricks (4-1-9). Some Nigerians are often unfairly judged by the world press, which rarely reports daily uphill and "against the wind" conditions in the country. Africa is a continent where the strong embrace life's treasures. Yet the impoverished seek to survive in the moment and pray to be strong by "next tomorrow".

Chapter Nine, **"Firm Foundation",** is an interesting read for CEO's and Professionals. It details our corporate challenges and the supreme effort it required as an American company to work in Nigeria, and succeed in a highly rewarding, mystical and demanding environment.

Chapter Ten, **"The Rich",** provides an explanation of what makes the Nigerian privileged class similar to other elite groups in the world, as well as what makes them uniquely different.

Chapter Eleven, **"You are Welcome",** is a brief, straightforward and, to the best of my knowledge, truthful assessment of many of the normal conditions that exist in the giant of Africa.

Chapter Twelve, **"'Divine' Purpose",** is for the esteemed readers, including scholars and intellectuals. The final chapter will allow the reader to visualize the author's full body of experiences; justifying the educational, humorous and spiritual conditions coming together to provide a hopeful solution, and spiritually powerful relevance.

I implore you to give "Who Turned off the Lights", a place in your soul and home. It is yours. Buy it and enjoy the author's true-life journey.

THEME

In the prime of his career, looking to expand his company's market, an ambitious CEO travels abroad and lands in a young democracy. Experience how the spiritual *'twine that binds'* provides a unified hope for a brighter future.

ACKNOWLEDGEMENTS

T o my wife Dr. Shondria Woods- McAfee, my son Alfonso McAfee III, my father Alfonso McAfee and Mother Reverend. Geneva E. McAfee (who gave so much love to me and so many others).

Mary H. Tolden, my Great Grandparents Charlie and Inez Austin, mother and father to Gertrude Austin Tolbert (John/Johnnie) and Mother and Father of Evelyna.

Grandparents Reverend Cassis   Mcfee, and Minnie Mcfee, Hugh "Green Eyes" Jones, Clarence "Papa" Rogers, Evelyna Rogers Tolbert and Levi Sullivan. My Great Uncle Pate   Mcfee, William   McAfee, Harmon Mcfee, Uncle Fred Hughes Mcfee (like a father), Larry Lipscomb, Willie C.   Mcfee, Leon Mcfee, Archie Mcfee, John   Mcfee, Robert Lay and Casey Mcfee.

Great Aunts Joyce Ford, Ola Adams, Eliza Davis Adams, Janis Lipscomb, Mary Barrington.

Aunts Willa Mae Sullivan, Izona Nichols, Betty Faye Mcfee, Ola Dean McAfee.

My brothers Derek Martin, Darryl Martin, Anthony D Martin, Vern Allen Martin, Dennis Mcfee, Robin Mcfee Wright, Adrian Mcfee, Stacey L. Mcfee.

Who Turned out the Lights?

My Sister Lesia Victoria Mcfee.

My cousins Denise Sullivan Hall, Bo Austin, Clarence Holiday Balls, Ricky Balls Holiday, Ira, John, Dexter, Tim, Lonnie Mcfee, Hugh, Tony, and Bruce Jones, Myra Gibbs, Michelle Neal, Sandra Neal, Rusty Neal Sullivan, Karen, Michael, Dennis, Anthony, Roderick Balls and Donald Vaughn.

Nephews Damione Williams, Kenyon, Adrian "Nana", Jr., Rico, Stacey, Jr. and Adrian "Loretta".

Nieces Tamara Martin, Tamaress, and Dawn.

For my family listed above, the world will know that you were here.

To Mrs. Teal, Liddell and Mr. Thomas, early age teachers that taught me well. Mrs. Carter, my high school counselor, who pushed and challenged me by enrolling me in the most difficult classes. My civic center coach Jerry Redeemer. Mr. Louis Oats, who had the most dramatic impact on my life, convincing me to explore out of State educational opportunities. Bob Timbrook, who introduced me to the corporate heads and opened up International Business opportunities.

John Damron, a man whom I can always count on to get things. Terrell Freeman, my college counselor and friend. Torrye Loveless, my college roommate, and Donas

Nesbitt, two friends who looked at life from a different perspective but allowed me to relish the good sides.

The following group consists of, but is not limited to, a select few of the many Nigerians that assisted me with jobs, security and advice on this book and surviving in the Giant of Africa:

Lloyd and Elems Ukwu, Robin Meja, Flexible, Christine "Madam Olele, Lousia Ayijaie, Femi Ogunbolude, Tunde Joseph, Friday Kindness, Chinwe & Chindera, Issac Ujogie, Governor Wada,_Chairman Atawodi, Captain Arome, Commander Atiku, Eric, Desmond, and Nanfa Fadip.

Finally, I must always remember to thank God, family and friends in Atlanta, Georgia for providing wisdom, safety and the strength to complete this most spiritual undertaking.

Who Turned out the Lights?

CHAPTER 1: THE SUN

A s a child I would often escape the company of my family and friends to find a place to meditate, and sleep outside in the back of our detached garage in the direct sunlight.

Born in Buena Vista Township, at 1857 North Outer Drive Saginaw, Michigan USA, we had very cold winters and very few hot sunny summer days.

I enjoyed waking up early in the morning to view the east sunrise through my window, which shone over the corn field across the road, just opposite of our house. My day ended by watching the sunset pass overhead going west in the evening.

Being the sixth child in a family with eight brothers and one sister, I had a very happy childhood. Because I had so many brothers, I was shielded from being bullied by outsiders, however, the fights that I had were to gain respect from members of my family. My eldest brother, in my eyes, was the perfect alpha male yet, he was quiet and strong. He was a protector of the family inside and outside of our home.

Each male sibling could posture himself after him in a confident manner, because they knew doing so would result in a sense of safety and security. It was this sense of security which allowed me to make decisions based on the good within me, which may have been acquired from the idle time spent absorbing rays of the sun. Similarly, my father was a strong and quiet man, as I remember. He died when I was only 9 years old.

I recall going out with my Dad in his old pickup truck one day. During that time wearing seat belts was not the law. Somehow, the passenger's side door was not fully closed so, as my Dad took a left turn at the corner, the passenger side door flung open and I was ejected from the old pickup truck. The truck took a hard left and I took a hard fall into our neighbor's gravel driveway.

My dad stopped, picked me up and rushed me back home. Upon arrival he explained to my Mother what happened and, in a loud and exciting tone, she replied ***"WHY DID YOU BRING HIM HOME? TAKE HIM TO THE HOSPITAL."*** After receiving medical attention for bumps and bruises I was just fine, but I could never figure out what the fuss was about. In another unrelated incident, my Dad closed the car door and it crushed the middle finger on my right hand. My Dad was not a clumsy man, nor was he a child abuser. In fact, I am certain that he loved me dearly.

However, it was just two unfortunate incidents that I have never forgotten. My dad never motivated me with words but he did so with a quiet look of confidence that radiated love, which felt like a direct ray of sunlight. My Uncle Fred later told me that, in his youth, my dad was very smart and a good athlete. As a Child, I was also considered among my peers as smart and athletic. I can still recall my first day of grade school, I harbored no childish fear. It was like a second home because all of my brothers were already there.

Our school was called Downs Elementary. It was a very basic built structure. In order to go from one classroom to the next, we would have to go outside. I can remember eating graham crackers, drinking milk and taking naps on my personal rug on my first day being dropped off by my mother. My first teacher's name was Mrs. Teal. She was a very old white lady teaching a majority black class. She was also very kind. After my kindergarten year, my first grade teacher was Mrs. Liddell. She taught me from the first to the fourth grade. I excelled in her classroom because I learned a lot at home from my older brothers Derek, Darryl, Anthony, Vern and Dennis.

I enjoyed school and I always looked forward to attending. I can recall being separated into a small group because we comprehended the lesson faster than the other students. Mrs. Liddell stressed math, reading and clarity of one's penmanship, which I worked hard to master. I also enjoyed writing numbers. This early practice helped me later in life with my performance in graphics and engineering. As a group, Mrs. Liddell challenged us daily and never expressed to us verbally that we were doing exemplary work.

Perhaps, it was to keep us humble or maybe she felt it was simply what was expected of us. After school while playing with my friends, I would run and tease the classroom bully because he was larger but slower. I ran very fast and I knew he could never catch me so, when our group was being chased, I would lag behind. I did this to encourage my friends to run faster, allowing the bully to chase me so that my slower friends could escape.

We lived in the country, but not on a farm. We had a large garden, a few chickens and a cow. My Dad was a builder. He purchased land which contained an old house that he tore down and remodeled using most of the same nails. I can recall, during my first construction job, straightening nails with my brothers Dennis, Bob (Robin), Adrian and Stacey for reuse. Even today when walking on my job sites, I pick up nails and put them in my pocket for later use. On weekends, my father would watch the white birds play the black birds, as the kids would call it. In reality, on our black and white television we really watched the Detroit Lions vs. the Chicago Bears. I remember Dad relaxing in his favorite chair, drinking a bottle of coke with peanuts inside. As an adult, similar to my Dad, I would relax in my favorite chair, often enjoying coke with peanuts and watching football. I guess, I am now a father, and many of my father's habits are infused in me.

My father and I went many places together however, we didn't talk much. I guess we had a spiritual understanding. He loved me and I understood his expression of love. Maybe it was God's way of preparing me to rely on my Dad's spiritual presence to guide me through life, because his physical presence was not ordained to remain. After the death of my father, tragedy struck my family again. My Mother's elder sister was killed in an auto accident leaving six children, my cousins. The senior daughter moved in with my grandfather, the youngest son moved in with his father and the other two boys and two girls moved into our house. Our family grew from ten to fourteen children overnight. One of my cousins, Sandra, was my age while the others were all older.

We all had a mutually respectful relationship during our years living together. Most of the time Sandra and I were in the same classroom. Then, all of a sudden, the girls moved out of town to their father's home in Flint, Michigan. The elder boys also moved out, but mainly stayed in Saginaw, MI.

Additionally, our house burned down due to an unknown problem. As a result of this, the family moved into the house remodeled by my dad along with the rental tenants, elderly married couple Dave and Martha, until the purchase of a new home months later at Three 40 Five. My mother endured the loss of her husband, elder sister, inherited four additional children and the loss of our house to a fire. She managed to keep the family together through her strength and the blessings received from GOD.

Through all of the mentioned hardships, I never understood until later in life why my sixth grade teacher was always so kind. He often asked how things were at home, and if I was ok. Maybe it was because I looked a bit untidy due to our hardship at home, but I never realized such because I ate well every day and my health was good. I also managed to keep excellent grades and was happy most of the time. When my Dad was around, he would always make sure our school lunches were paid, and that each child got a weekly allowance. After his passing, we shifted to a government paid lunch program, which caused me to feel embarrassed daily.

I can recall every day, during my entire sixth grade year, adjusting my place in the lunch line away from my friends. When the time came for me to pay, I would tell the cashier that my Mom or Dad had already paid for my lunch; in fact it was my Uncle Sam (US Government). I remember the cashier being so understanding. She would always smile, nod and let me pass.

Looking back as an adult, I realized no one in America deserved government assistance more than our family, considering my father was a veteran of a foreign war, and lost his life in a tragic accident working for the General Motors (GM), leaving a wife and ten children.

My most memorable elementary school event was when our class sold caramel apples for the entire year, fundraising for our trip to Greenfield Village in Detroit, the home of the Ford Model A car. Our return trip back to Saginaw was by Air. This was my first flight at the age of ten and it was the experience that erased all my fears of flying, and prepared me for my future, international travel.

The sun is the Star, located in the center of our solar system. It is 109 times bigger than our planet Mass is about 330,000 times that of Earth.

Mysterious and enormous, the sun attracts our attention and inspires us at times when we are looking for the light...

"Happiness can be found in the Darkest of Times, when one only Remembers To turn on the Light."

-Albus Dumbledore

Who Turned out the Lights?

"When the sun is shining I can do anything; no mountain too high, no trouble too difficult to overcome."

- Wilma Rudolph

CHAPTER 2: THREE 40 FIVE

After completion of the Sixth grade, our family moved into our new home bearing the address number 345. It would be the house where I came of age and began to explore all things in the life of a growing boy (playing, working, loving, and loss).

Upon entering middle school, I noticed a sharp drop in my math grades and an accelerated interest in other courses. However, it was math and science which would be my true calling. Perhaps it was because of my new location, new environment or just growing pains that I didn't apply myself fully, but I never lost my mathematical fundamentals, a process that would be instrumental in my educational pursuit in engineering.

Additionally, I received my first job as a paperboy for the Saginaw News. Initially, I began as an assistant to the primary guy Bruce, and later I took over his route as he moved on. At the age of twelve, having a job allowed me some financial independence. More importantly, I got to know every one of my neighbors personally. Unlike my friends, I was able to tap into the wisdom, kindness, and history of the elders in my neighborhood.

The African proverb that says, "It takes a village to raise a child" came to fruition in my life. Neighbors would invite me to have a cup of hot chocolate on a cold winter day, or a place to ride out the storm on a rainy day. Or just to sit and listen to life's memories from a lonely widow while I waited to find out when I would get paid. I knew the teachers, factory workers, businessmen and women. I was also exposed to the heavy drinkers in my community.

I was considered a humble, listening ear when my neighbors spoke with me. The wisdom and guidance from my neighbor's young, old, white, black, Spanish, male, female, healthy and sick all helped to mold, and equip me with a unique gift to access strangers. I have always felt obliged to look deeper than the flesh to discover the inner spirit of people.

When it came to middle school, most kids felt socialization was more important than getting good grades. Middle school was a very critical mental growth period of a child's life, as this is a time when one begins to develop certain traits or patterns that may determine if he or she becomes a leader or a follower. I was not a popular kid in school and I didn't feel particularly liked by girls or the school jocks.

The popular guys dressed up every day and wanted to insult, influence and control you, so I picked my own set of nerdy cool friends. One short, one tall and one Mexican and, among them all, I was the cool kid. I thought I was somehow the leader of the group because I made my own decisions and wasn't afraid to "just say no" to drugs, cigarettes, alcohol, cutting class or any other thing I didn't like or want to do. Although Shorty (Calvin) was a ladies man, we all enjoyed our school work and loved sports. My friends gave me a place of pride and assurance. I can attest we were not concerned with what popular kids in school thought of us, therefore, I matured with confidence. My second job was with the McDonalds Corporation, during my high school years. It was hard work, but it taught me about the importance of cleanliness. Years later as a father I would always tell my son:

"A clean person can live anywhere

A dirty person can only live somewhere"

- *Goodwill Ambassador Al McAfee, Jr.*
As a man thinks he is…

If you think you can do something you can

If you think that you can't you're right

-Goodwill Ambassador Al McAfee, Jr.

During my employment at McDonalds, I felt embarrassed whenever my friends would come inside and see me cleaning tables in the lobby, picking up trash in the parking lot and dumping trash. Even at a young age

Who Turned out the Lights?

I felt I was always better, and that others should be doing these low level chores. So I learned to cook and was promoted to working in the kitchen. I was able to stay in the kitchen where I had the ability to be in control of something, even if it was just the flow of food. More importantly, I would never be asked to tend to the lot and lobby again.

Our childhood social activities included football, basketball, baseball, roller skating and ice hockey. As far as team sports, we fielded a Saginaw, Michigan city baseball, basketball and flag football Team league. Some of the best baseball talent in our neighborhood would go over to the west side and play with the white guys, and clean our clocks in summer league baseball games. But our football and basketball teams had no problem competing. I was born in the month of November, the flag football fifteen and under league was from September to December. I was the quarterback on the team but I was removed in pre-season by league officials, because I would've turned sixteen before the end of the season.

Consequently, I decided to establish a new team where I would be head coach with the assistance of my third elder brother, Anthony, who would be the adult present at the games. After securing funds for uniforms and fee's from the parent of one of our players who sponsored us, his dad was a General Motors (GM) union committeeman, we respectfully named the team United Action Local 455. Although young with no prior coaching experience, we competed competitively every game, finishing in second place two years in a row in City league play.

High school was fun and my group of friends loved to compete academically. Our counselors would provide the most challenging courses to get us college ready. I recall sitting in physics class with four or five other students when a kid opened our door, threw a book inside and ran down the hall shouting "Bookworms! Bookworms!" There was this girl Vicky that I adored who was in my college writing class.

One day at home while doing my homework for Mr. Pratt's college writing course, Vicky showed up at our house to see my brother Vern. She noticed me and asked me what I was doing. When I told her college writing homework, she laughed and shouted, "Do you actually do that shit?" Additionally, one of the school jocks approached me and asked why, as a good athlete, didn't I play with the school's sports teams?

I was good enough but my family lacked the connections needed to play on sports teams in my high school, however, I was connected academically. The name of our school was Saginaw High. The "High" was known as a basketball powerhouse school and competed against all the class A schools in the State. My senior year we could have played against the National Basketball Association (NBA) superstar Magic Johnson's high school, Lansing Everett, but Magic's school lost in the semifinals to Detroit Catholic Central. And we eventually lost to Detroit Catholic Central in the State Championship game.

In my junior year in high school the General Motors Corporation and the Dow Chemical Company jointly decided to increase minority engineers in their workforce. So for two years they provided pre-engineering scholarship/grants to promising minority students across the state of Michigan. John, my Mexican friend, and myself were two of the students selected from our school. I am not sure of the actual count of scholarships/grants offered, but after graduation I was invited back to Saginaw, and compensated to give a motivational speech to Delta college minority students. This opportunity was presented to me after learning that I was the only member of the engineering scholarship group to finish with a degree in engineering.

The program was discontinued shortly thereafter. So, to answer the jocks question regarding my commitment to the School …Yes! I represented our school against some of the States brightest students, not as a jock, but in a cerebral competition. Therefore, (I was) in my humble opinion, I was a high school first team academic All State student representing the "High".

Furthermore, I somehow felt thirty years after our high school days, when the jocks are in physical decline, I will be in my mental prime.

During my college career I met and befriended a member of the royal family of a Middle Eastern Country. I often wondered why one would choose a small college in a mid-Michigan community to attend school. After investigating this, I noticed that the small oil rich Middle Eastern country has a very similar shape as the state of Michigan. So much of my initial academic student relationships began with a group of friends from the Middle East.

The following year I transferred to Florida A & M University in Tallahassee, Florida. Inspired by my mother's interest, I considered going into the Pharmacology program. However, after being caught and exposed for allowing my friend to cheat off my paper during a chemistry final exam, we were both kicked out of class and I received a failing grade. I quickly changed my major and mindset back to engineering.

The engineering school was isolated from the main campus. Although the institution was a Historically Black College and University (HBCU), the technical school consisted mostly of foreign faculty with Ph.D.'s and a diverse international student body. By my second year, after being involved in political and social matters, I was nominated and voted in to become the student

Who Turned out the Lights?

President of the schools American Society of Civil Engineers (ASCE) by the students.

My best friend was a brilliant engineering student by the name of Pitpaul Daiuwal from India. He also happened to be the nephew of the Chairman of the Engineering Department. My extended list of international friends in the engineering school included, Eggbal Jaylalee from Iran, Obi from Kenya, Adrishar Komanadidote from Iran, and Fradune from Beirut, Lebanon. My roommate, whose mom made the best homemade oatmeal raisin cookies, and I would often travel to Daytona Beach with our Florida State University friends during Spring Break. We would stay at our friend Scott's parents' house, whose dad was Vice Chairman of major Aeronautical University.

At that university, American Engineers and Pilots studied for the space program and airline industry. Rather than traveling back to Michigan for Spring Break, we chose to hang out with Florida Daytona beach kids that loved basketball and dare devil activities. These activities included things such as cliff diving in a remote location in the dead of night, water skiing in the river while being pulled by a speed boat, and body surfing in the Atlantic Ocean.

The two or three times I have been totally wasted in my life was in Tallahassee bars with my Florida beach boy friends. Additionally, being a northerner (Yankee), my friend from Lakeland, Florida taught me a lot about Southern lore. His dad told such memorable jokes that, to this day, I often recite them. Through these relationships I would sharpen my understanding of people both foreign and domestic. I acquired a greater understanding and respect for others customs, traditions and politics, which fundamentally prepared me for international business.

Upon Graduation, I returned home to Saginaw. The economy was in a recession so I took a job on the Boblo boat on downtown Detroit's riverfront as a security guard. I did this just until I was able to secure my first engineering related position with the Saginaw County Government. The previous owner of the home we moved into at 345, who was now a member of the county road commission board, gave me a good recommendation. The job was the worst, in my humble opinion, because the employees were nice nasty, there was no training program to speak of and whenever I did something well even without training, they moved me on to something else.

If ever there was a job I wanted to go postal on it was this job. I remember being harassed during a surprise surveying test exercise by my supervisor, who never spent one hour in the field with me, until I went home with bloodshot red eyes. Days later I was fired. As opposed to taking up arms, I promised myself if I ever had an opportunity to supervise anyone, I would never treat any person the way I was treated. Once again, I left Saginaw, Michigan and returned to the South. Arriving in Atlanta, Georgia the economy was a buzz. I met a surveyor for an engineering firm during a gas stop and he informed me that his company was hiring.

The next day I went in for an interview and was hired on the spot. I never unpacked my car but I had a job and was ready to begin a new chapter in my life. My first months working with the consulting engineering firm was a good learning experience. I recall asking one of the landscape architects a question. He came back one hour later with an answer and eventually billed my department for his time, although we worked for the same firm. Within two years, I acquired knowledge in highway, bridge and railroad engineering. Later, I interviewed for an engineering position with a British owned steel Corporation and, after a few weeks on the job, I was promoted by the British to a Project Management position.

I reported directly to the President. My responsibilities included the overall management of a new steel product called "Steelguard", which was used in place of reinforcing steel bars (rebar) to secure money in bank vaults. Within one year, I sold, designed and shipped Steelguard for over 123 bank vault construction projects in the United States. Although the vault program was successful, the company went out of business thirteen months later. The British suggested that I establish my own firm because I had solid contacts within the banking industry. With my $2,000.00 USD severance pay, I established McAfee Design & Distributing Co., Inc., in Atlanta, Georgia.

During my first ten years in business my brothers Adrian, Robin (Bob), Stacey our superintendent, ((Charles "Dad "Smith)) and I designed, shipped, and constructed over 1,000 bank vaults in America. We also completed subcontracting work on the following: Georgia Dome Football Stadium, the Memphis Internal Revenue Service Center, the Gwinnett County Civic and Cultural Center, the Marta Railway Bridge over Georgia 400, the Jimmy Dyess Parkway from Fort Gordon Military Installation to Interstate 20, and the bridge from Marathon Island to Key West Florida. McAfee Design and Distributing Co., Inc. was awarded the 1994 City of Atlanta Minority Construction Firm of the year. We acquired the Outstanding Business letter of recognition in the State of Georgia.

We were also nominated and presided over a case for the American Association of Arbitrators. We appeared on television interviews with People TV and Channel 5 Good Day Atlanta. I accepted a Goodwill Ambassadorship appointment from the Secretary of State of Georgia. We also earned the Trailblazer of the year award City of Atlanta and appeared on the Cover of

Who Turned out the Lights?

September 1997 magazine The Atlanta Tribune. We were awarded the National Minority Construction Firm of the year 1997, and we collected a Scholarship/Grant to Ivy League school Dartmouth College from the US Commence Department under the Clinton administration.

More important than any other blessing from GOD, was me being in good health. Reflecting back on my life's honors, I am amazed at how God prepares one to do his will. Whether home or abroad, as long as I am alive, I will never forget my childhood experiences at 1857 North Outer Drive, or my youthful days living and learning at Three 40 Five.

"The will of God will never lead you where the Grace of God cannot keep you."

-Bishop Dale C. Bronner

Alfonso McAfee is part of an elite group of successful entrepreneurs in America who has prospered in the market-place by making it their own personal oyster. McAfee "pearls" can be found in (the) hundreds of locations throughout the country in high security areas, where our nation's top businesses are willing to pay premium dollars for a product that secures its assets.

Like other giants in the industry, McAfee has a unique offering that he has fine tuned into a successful marketing niche. Like most successful marketers, he has been able to diversify and grow his product line with new-age technology in a changing marketplace that keeps his Company, McAfee Design & Distributing Co. Inc., at the cutting edge and a step ahead of the competition. McAfee builds state of the art vaults that are the "best-in-the industry" and the cornerstone of banks, financial institutions and high–level executive offices. There are only a handful of entrepreneurs in the country who provide the services, and none do it at a lower cost with better quality and more expertise.

McAfee's ingenuity has earned him the 1997 Trailblazer of the year Award presented in September, during Minority Enterprise Development week, by the U.S. Department of Commerce, Minority Business Development Agency, and Atlanta Regional office.

McAfee, like most successful businessmen, has honed his focus on growing his company, expanding the bottom line, and marketing to clients who cannot live without his product.

- By Yao Atilm Seidu "The Atlanta Tribune"

"Leaving home to me means following God's plan in pursuit of his will for your life, which is more vital than the pursuit of what your family, society or your home tells you is important."

-Goodwill Ambassador Al McAfee, Jr.

Who Turned out the Lights?

CHAPTER 3: AFRICA

In one word, the continent of Africa is BIG. 100% of the way in which the size of the continent is viewed in relationship to other countries is inaccurate. In fact, the land mass is equal to all of Europe and Russia. Africa in total is more than 30 million square kilometers.

AFRICA

In a word the continent of Africa is BIG. One Hundred percent of the way in which the size of the continent is viewed in relationship to other countries is accurate.

In fact the land mass is equal to all of Europe and Russia. Africa in total is more than 30 million square kilometers see attached photos.

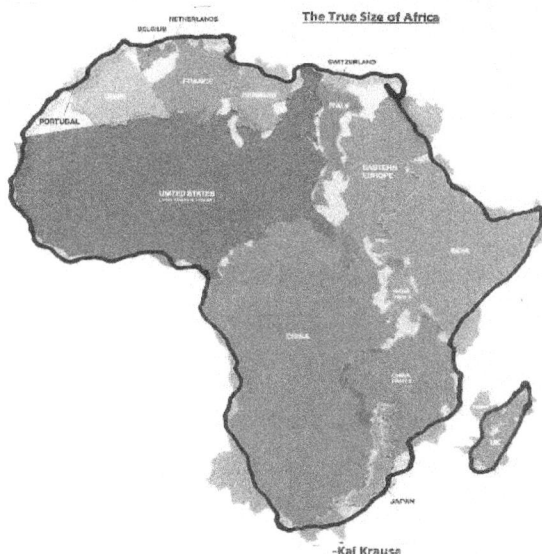

The True Size of Africa

-Kai Krause

14

43

Please note, most graphics illustrates that its size is not shown accurately on a standard Mercator Map, where countries in the center appear smaller than they are. This graphic shows Africa is bigger than the land masses of the US, China, India, Mexico, Peru, France, Spain, Papua New Guinea, Sweden, Japan, Germany, Norway, Italy, New Zealand, the UK, Nepal, Bangladesh and Greece put together.

-Kai Krause

Just the facts: Every Americans Should Know

➢ Africa is the most populous and the only black continent.

➢ Africa is often referred to, and also known as the "Mother Land". As all proof shows information provided by human origin, early humans first migrated out of Africa into Asia between 1.8 to 2 million years ago. It is also considered to be the cradle of civilization.

➢ The original name of Africa was said to be known as 'Alkebulan', the land of the Blacks and "Mother of Mankind" or" Garden of Eden."-quora.com world atlas articles May 20, 2018

Who Turned out the Lights?

➢ Many people, especially American, do not realize the continent of Africa is made up of 58 different countries which include Egypt, Morocco, Equatorial Guinea, Libya and Madagascar.

➢ In 2001, George W. Bush famously commented that, "Africa is a nation that suffers from terrible disease", thereby reducing the planet's second-largest continent to a single country.

Rank by land mass: List of 58 independent African countries with different national Flags

1. Algeria

2. Democratic Republic of the Congo

3. Sudan

4. Libya

5. Chad

6. Niger

7. Angola

8. Mali

9. South Africa

Who Turned out the Lights?

10. Ethiopia

11. Mauritania

12. Egypt

13. Tanzania

14. Nigeria

15. Namibia

16. Mozambique

17. Zambia

18. South Sudan

19. Somalia

20. Central African Republic

21. Botswana

22. Madagascar

23. Kenya

24. Cameroon

25. Morocco

26. Zimbabwe

27. Republic of Congo

Who Turned out the Lights?

28. Ivory Coast

29. Burkina Faso

30. Gabon

31. Western Sahara

32. Guinea

33. Ghana

34. Uganda

35. Senegal

36. Tunisia

37. Eritrea

38. Malawi

39. Benin

40. Liberia

41. Sierra Leone

42. Togo

43. Guinea- Bissau

44. Lesotho

45. Equatorial Guinea

46. Burundi

47. Rwanda

48. Djibouti

49. Eswatini

50. Gambia

51. Cape Verde

52. Reunion

53. Comoros

54. Mauritius

55. Sao Tome and Principe

56. Seychelles

57. Saint Helena

58. Mayotte

Who Turned out the Lights?

-Geoba Gazetteer

- ➢ Madagascar, an independent African country, is the 4th largest Island in the world. Often, Westerners make the mistake of thinking the continents' history began with the arrival of colonial explorers to sub-Saharan Africa in the 15th century. In the 12th century, while Oxford and Cambridge Universities were in their infancy, Timbuktu in Mali already had three thriving Universities and more than 180 Quranic schools. Moreover, Timbuktu, Mali is home of the oldest universities in the world, established in 982 CE.
- ➢ Liberia is a country established by American slaves.
- ➢ Ethiopia is the only African country with its own alphabet.
- ➢ Sudan has more than 200 pyramids, double the number in Egypt.
- ➢ Islam is the most dominant religion in Africa, followed by Christianity.
- ➢ Under Gaddafi, former African leader of Libya before the fall of Tripoli(,) and his untimely demise, Gaddafi was trying to introduce a single African currency linked to gold, following in the footsteps of the late Marcus Garvey who first coined the term "United States of Africa". Gaddafi wanted to introduce

and only trade in the African gold Dinar, -a move which would have thrown the world economy into chaos. The Dinar was widely opposed by the 'elite' of today's society, and who could blame them. *African nations would have finally had the power to bring itself out of debt and poverty, and only trade in this precious commodity. They would have been able to say 'no' to external exploitation, and charge whatever they felt suitable for precious resources.*

➢ It has been said that the gold Dinar was the real reason for the NATO led rebellion, in a bid to oust the outspoken leader.

➢ Gaddafi, at the time of his death, was worth over 200 Billion in cash and assets.

➢ Libya had no external debt and had reserves of $150 billion, which was frozen globally. Meanwhile, the USA had a debt of over $18 Trillion. Libya under Gaddafi had none.

➢ -The African Exponent https://twitter.com/intent/tweet? url=https%3A%2F%2Fwww.africanexponet.c om% 2F post%2Ften-reasons-libya-under-gaddafi-was-a-great-place-to-live-2746&via=africanexponet

➢ Mansa Musal Net Worth: 400 Billion amongst many other titles, Mansa Musa.

Who Turned out the Lights?

- The lord of the mines of Wangara was the 10th emperor of the Malian Empire. He is the wealthiest to have ever lived in human history. The devout Muslim wielded so much power and controlled a lot of wealth in the early 14th century. He ruled over 400 cities of Mali, then the whole of West Africa, for 25 years. He founded the University of Sankore in Timbuktu. He also benefited from the exports of gold and salt -Sergio Domian Answers Africa

- Mosquitoes can transmit numerous dangerous diseases, such as malaria, and kill most people.

- The Puff Adder is the most dangerous snake.

- Africa has the largest desert, the Sahara, which is almost the same size as the United States.

- Between 1525 and 1866, 12.5 million Africans were kidnaped and sold into slavery in the Americas.

- The African hippopotamus is unbelievably responsible for more human deaths in Africa than any other large animal, not lions, tigers, and snakes as we have come to believe.

- Bantu Stephen Biko was a South African anti-Apartheid activist. Biko founded the Black Consciousness movement of the 1960s. In 2002, Nelson Mandela said of Biko, "Living, he was the spark that lit a veld fire across South

Africa." His message to the youth and students was simple and clear, "Black is Beautiful! Be proud of your Blackness!" He inspired our youth to shed themselves of the sense of inferiority they were born into as a result of more than three hundred years of white rule".
– Independent

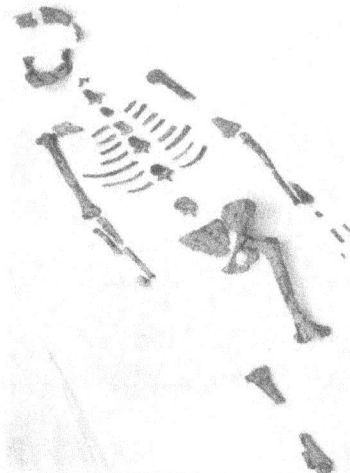

The skeleton of "Lucy", a hominid who lived approximately 3.2 million years ago identified in 1974 and has been considered a common ancestor of the human family. This jaw-dropping discovery took place in Hadar, Ethiopia. Additionally, in 1979, a 165 foot trail of the earliest hominid footprints was discovered in the Kibish region of Tanzania, with these facts, North-Eastern Africa was marked as the birthplace of humanity.

The skeleton of "Lucy", a hominid that lived approximately 3.2 million years ago, was identified in 1974 and has been considered a common ancestor of the human family. This jaw- dropping discovery took place in Hadar, Ethiopia. Additionally, in 1979, a 165 foot trail of the earliest hominid footprints was discovered in the Kibish region of Tanzania. With these facts, North-Eastern Africa was marked as the birthplace of humanity.

➤ The Pan African Christian Church bestowed upon the Author the African name: Bilal

Mawuli Motilewa meaning: ("a black Man" "there is a God" "I am from Home")

➤ Ameyoh Stella Shade Adadevoh (October 27, 1956 – August 19, 2014) was a Nigerian doctor who oversaw the treatment of Patrick Sawyer, the Liberian National who brought the Ebola virus to Nigeria. The first doctor at First Consultants Medical Centre (FCMC) who saw Mr. Sawyer diagnosed him with malaria. When Dr. Adadevoh saw him during her ward rounds the following day, she suspected Ebola despite the initial malaria diagnosis and the fact that neither she, nor any other doctor in Nigeria, had ever seen Ebola before. In 2012, when swine flu spread to Lagos, Adadevoh was the first doctor to diagnose and alert the Ministry of Health. Less than 2 years later in 2014, she was again the first doctor to identify another contagious virus-Ebola. Additionally, she was the one who stopped the late American Liberian Patrick Sawyer when he removed his drip tube and tried to leave the hospital. He became violent, but Dr. Adadevoh used force and was able to stop him. She took it upon herself to help Nigeria prevent further spread of the virus as she took the case to the government. Dr. Adadevoh's accurate and swift diagnosis of Sawyer resulted in the

Nigerian government mobilizing the necessary resources to deal with an Ebola outbreak. Dr. Adadevoh's sacrifice prevented a *national, or possibly global, catastrophe.* If Sawyer succeeded in forcing himself out of the hospital, it would have been difficult to trace those who had contact with him. When threatened by Liberian officials who wanted the patient to be discharged to attend a conference, she resisted the pressure and said, "For the greater public good" she would not release him. There were 20 Ebola cases in total. Eleven were healthcare workers and, of those healthcare workers, 6 survived and 5 died, including Dr. Adadevoh. In her last moments she received intravenous fluids and oxygen support, and was being monitored closely by doctors from the World Health Organization (WHO). Eventually, she died of the virus on August 19, 2014. She was 57. Her heroic and patriotic deeds will never be forgotten. A true Nigerian Hero.

➢ Bennet Ifeakandu Omalu, born September 1968, is a Nigerian-American physician, forensic pathologist, and neuropathologist who was the first to discover and publish findings of chronic traumatic encephalopathy (CTE) in American football players. While working at the Allegheny County coroner's office in Pittsburgh, my son and his friend co-organized a conference to bring the finding of (CTE), founded by Dr. Omalu, to the attention of the football loving communities in Atlanta, Georgia.

➢ Many of the awards and honorary degrees given to former South African President Nelson Mandela, by American HBCU's, are proudly displayed in his home in Johannesburg, South Africa. I am sure of this as my wife and I have visited his early life family home, and bear witness.

➢ Former Zimbabwe President Robert Gabriel Mugabe talked about systematic genocide of Black Americans.

➢ Zimbabwe, one of the poorest countries in Africa, is the only country in the world where almost everyone was a billionaire at one point. Zimbabwe Reserve bank printed a $21 trillion bill to pay off debts owed to the International Monetary Fund.

-Facts about Africa

For those Americans that have been taken in by the "propaganda" regarding the continent of Africa and its people. I hope by detailing my experiences through years of travel to the Mother Land, you will realize that Africa is a beautiful, dynamic, peaceful, and troubling place. However, just like any other country that is not your native land, danger exists primarily out of ignorance. But I hope to provide relevant information to ensure a greater understanding of Africa and the country of Nigeria in particular.

Additionally, I would like to make it abundantly clear that my observations are from the thoughts, ideals, upbringing and eyes of a humble and right-minded American citizen. Some Americans, Nigerians, and other Africans may beg to differ but I am calling things as I see them, and I am sure other black American's would concur.

If President Obama wants me to allow marriage for same sex couples in my country (Zimbabwe), he must come here so that I marry him first."

- Robert Mugabe Former President of Zimbabwe

As of August 30, 2019 Chibok Girls: 106 OUT, 112 to GO, we pray for the safe return of all our sisters. "The missing girls should not be forgotten".

- Goodwill Ambassador Al McAfee, Jr.

Who Turned out the Lights?

Propaganda - Information, ideas, opinions, or images often only giving one part of an argument, that are broadcast, published or in some way spread with the intentions of influencing people's opinions:

-Webster's Dictionary

"The truth is the best picture, the best propaganda".

-Robert Capa

The most effective way to destroy people is to deny and obliterate their own understanding of their history".

-George Orwell

Who Turned out the Lights?

CHAPTER 4: THE GIANT OF AFRICA

Nigeria is the most populated country in the continent of Africa thus it is often called the "Giant of Africa". With a population of over 210 million people, the country has over 200 different languages. However, the official language is English.

There are over 250 different tribes in Nigeria. The three major tribes encompasses 60% of the population, mainly Muslim (Hausa and Fulani) in the North. Mainly Christian Igbo's live in the south east and Yorubas in the South West. The six most significant ethnic groups will include Efik-Ibibio and Edo. Nigeria is an oil rich country blessed with an abundance of essential natural resources, and with fertile land. In my humble opinion, the land is "magical", producing every type of nutritious fruit and vegetables, especially in the Niger Delta south-south region.

My first visit to the continent was in November of 1999. To reach our final destination, it required a direct flight from New York City to the country of Ghana. When we landed, I felt a simple feeling of relief. It could have been the spirits of my ancestors welcoming me back, or perhaps just the smooth and professional landing after twelve hours in the air by the Ghanaian Airline pilots.

Who Turned out the Lights?

We arrived in Ghana's Capital City, Accra. During our one-day layover we didn't see much of the country, but I noticed the hotel was decent. The city was clean and appeared to be orderly, quiet and Ghanaians were serene and welcoming people.

The next day we departed to the Country of Nigeria, landing in one of the most populated cities in the world Lagos. We arrived around five o'clock pm. After about two hours on the ground, the first thing I concluded from the customs agents, baggage handlers, cab drivers, money changers and police is that Nigerians are loud, aggressive, soft spoken, cunning, and clever. Departing from the airport, our group took a long trip to our hotel in Victoria Island (VI).

In order to get there we had to pass through the Oshodi/Isolo Local Government Area (LGA). (,) Being an American, I must admit, the city of Lagos after dark in 1999 was shocking. The streets were lined with trash piled 10 to 15 feet high. The *"hold up or go slow"* was nerve wrecking and it also allowed young hawkers in the middle of the road to meander between cars aggressively, selling all types of cheap Chinese goods, and gadgets. There were pre-elementary school aged children begging for food, water, and money who had the ability to pray for you with the eloquence of an American mega church Bishop.

Who Turned out the Lights?

We noticed two Nigerians hanging out of both sides of a minivan transport bus with no doors, pointing flash lights at the road ahead, as the vehicle had no headlights. In fact, much of the city was in darkness. I now have some insight as to why astronauts on the international space station look down on earth and refer to Africa as the Dark Continent. Almost every truck on the road was emitting heavy smoke- and loud smog producing generators were everywhere. Thankfully they provide some light because, without them, moonlight would have been the only illumination.

Most cabs on the road looked as if they had hit everything but the state of Michigan lottery. Potholes are in the road everywhere and there were so many people crowding the streets that I felt, if you threw sand in the air, not one grain would hit the ground. I had been on the ground for two days and had not called my family to inform anyone of my safe arrival. I was about to pray, not to God, but to Scotty from Star Trek to beam me up. I can recall looking over at the expression on my American colleague's face and it appeared he didn't close his mouth until we reached Victoria Island, a more upscale section of Lagos side of the bridge.

After crossing the 11.8 kilometer (7.332 miles) third mainland bridge, which appeared to me at night to have been constructed just a quarter inch above the water line coming in from the high seas, we arrived at Bee Jay's Hotel in Victoria Island. After settling in, we ordered our first Nigerian meal, some kind of soup and Fufu. After biting into my first spoon full, all I can remember was a mad rush to the toilet to spit out the Fufu. It would take me another seven years before I tried Fufu again. After selecting another meal of chicken and rice and still being unable to make a call home, we retired for the night. I must confess on the first morning, after my first night of my first visit to Nigeria, I wept.

The next day I was able to make a ten dollar three minute call home. Shortly thereafter, we departed on our road trip from Lagos to Enugu. This was my first experience seeing a Nigerian military checkpoint. It kind of goes like this; imagine you're laid back cruising down the highway in a brand new double white Mercedes Benz, enjoying the beautiful Nigerian countryside, listening to some R. Kelly and Kenny Rogers on CD. All of a sudden you look up and see that the road is blocked with certain bushes, items, tree branches, etc...

You then notice five or six tall menacing looking Military Police carrying Ak-47 rifles. (One of them motioned the driver to stop the car. After about 20 minutes of checking the driver's particulars (paperwork) and a thorough search of the car, we were allowed to continue on our journey. It was later explained to us that the checkpoints operations is a method used to combat armed robbers and other criminals.

Nigerian highways have certain stretches of good pavement but far too many bad spots (potholes), which will cause a vehicle to nearly come to a full stop to get around them. During such a stop, this is where armed robbers would attack, so the driver is always on high alert. Additionally, this is also the perfect location for locals to come to the main highway to sell goods to passengers.

Their presence also provides travelers a sense of safety, and a way of providing food and drinks to travelers while still on the move. Moreover, if there is any blockage in the road, you don't see police, military or the local vigilante group acting on it. Stopping is not recommended. In fact, just the site of a vacant road block will cause an experienced Nigerian driver to immediately take aggressive action such as evading the obstruction, crashing through the roadblock or crossing over the median to the other side, (no need to be too alarmed).

Nigerian drivers are always on the lookout for vehicles traveling in the wrong direction as a sign of road construction, a severe section of bad roads or impending danger ahead. It is better to keep moving and risk an accident than to be captured by bandits in the countryside (bush). Thank God as all this madness was going on during our journey. My American partner and I were unaware of the danger. Hours later we would arrive safely to the Capital city of Enugu. In Enugu State we were received by a personal friend of our Nigerian host, Chief Ralph. Chief was a tall, stately gentleman who spoke perfect Queen's English, not to mention he was a Howard University (HBCU) graduate. We were both born on the same day and (on) this particular day just happened to be our birthday. Chief Ralph treated the group to a fine Chinese dinner and one day of complimentary accommodations at his hotel.

The following day we continued our trip to the "Garden City" of Port Harcourt, Capital of Rivers State and the number one oil revenue generating State in the Nation. Here we would pay our respects to the local Eze ROR, have a hearty meal, collect a Ghana *must go* bag of cash and be on our way to Bayelsa State and our final destination to meet the Governor.

On the road to Bayelsa state we were able to purchase some of the sweetest bananas, which go very well when taken with ground nuts (peanuts), fresh fish and snail (if your palette is up to the task). There was only one major road into the state at the time, and the Governor always traveled with a small army of security forces and an ambulance. Bayelsa State, like Rivers State, was also a major oil revenue producing State for the country. Inhabited dominantly by the Ijaw tribe, its nickname was "The Glory of all Lands".

Who Turned out the Lights?

It has water everywhere. The capital and largest city is Yenagoa. The first night we spent was dark, quiet and peaceful but it looked like we had just reached the end of the world. The next day we met His Excellency, the Governor, and our meeting went very well. (,) It lasted about two hours and ended with a group photo session with the Governor, as he embraced our efforts to bring American technology to his State. We returned to the City of Port Harcourt after our visit to the Bayelsa State House, which is where I held a press conference at our hotel. The article is attached below.

Page 6   INDEPENDENT MONITOR   November 27-29, 2000

NEWS

2003 GOVERNORSHIP ELECTIONS

US Engineering Coy Comes To Nigeria

The Chief Executive of a USA-based Engineering Construction Company, Mr Al Mcafee Jr, has set machineries in motion to transfer his modified American Construction Engineering works to Nigeria.

Mr Al-Mcafee disclosed in a chat with newsmen in Port Harcourt, stressing that he has the interest of Nigeria at heart and would practically demonstrate it by establishing an engineering construction company that would help provide employment opportunities to the youths.

He also intimated that he has as his focus the need to train Nigerian Engineering Students and equip them with technological know-how.

Mr Mcafee who bagged the 1997 outstanding businessman of the year award in Georgia and USA 1997 National Minority Construction firm of the year, equally enumerated some projects undertaken and completed by his company. They include Georgia Dome Football Stadium, RM Clayton Waste Water Treatment Plant, Metropolitan Atlanta Rapid Transportation Authority Train Bridge, and Eaglehart Special Metals and Diamond Vault.

Also contributing at the briefing, Dr Lloyd Ukwu, an indigene of Ekpeye Kingdom Rivers State expressed confidence in the ability of Mr Al Mcafee and his company and justified their ratings.

65

Who Turned out the Lights?

Port Harcourt after our visit to the Bayelsa State House where I held a press conference at our hotel the article is attached below.

US contractor hails Nigeria

THE efforts of the Federal Government to attract foreign investment to Nigeria has recorded a major dividend with the arrival in Nigeria of the first US construction company, Mcafee Inc. The president of Mcafee Inc., Mr. Alfonso Mcafee, made the observation in a chat with the News Agency of Nigeria (NAN) in Port Harcourt over the weekend.

He said that the new democratic environment in the country had rekindled the wave of investment interest among American businessmen toward Nigeria.

"After Clinton's visit to Nigeria, we were encouraged by the president to seize the opportunities offered by the prevalent democratic environment which had opened a window for investment in Nigeria," he said.

Mcafee, who said that his company would for now concentrate on road and bridge construction, expressed his intention to bring new technology to Nigeria.

"By the new technology, we intend to take undergraduates of engineering from some Nigerian universities as well as engineering graduates to the US and retrain them and bring them back home to work for us here," he said.

He further said that the new technology also emphasized speed and quality in project implementation, adding that Nigerians had been "paying 1960s jobs with 2000 money price".

"We are, therefore, set to give the country value for its investment in roads and bridges' construction," he added.

Mr. Lloyal Uknou, a member of the investment team, noted Nigeria's bias for roads and bridges' construction, and emphasis on quality and speed, saying that it was based on the realisation that no industry would survive without good roads.

My second trip to Nigeria was in January of 2001 It lasted about five months much of the time was spent in Port Harcourt Rivers State where my hotel was based we took several trips weekly to Bayelsa and other towns and villages seeking contracts. During our many

25

My second trip to Nigeria was in January of 2001. It lasted about five months. Much of the time was spent in Port Harcourt Rivers State, where my hotel was based. We took several trips weekly to Bayelsa, and other towns and villages seeking contracts. During several visits, I became close to the Bayelsa Governor, along with certain members of his administration. We never knew that, years later, this group headed by the former Deputy Governor would become leader of the Nigeria people.

Who Turned out the Lights?

This is also the period where I came of age in my experiences and developed a greater understanding of the African people, culture and traditions, especially of Nigerians. I became aware that the major difference between the continent of Africa and all the other places in the world I visited, is that Africans strongly believe and know how to utilize the power of GOD. Similarly, many Africans strongly believe in fear and know how to utilize the power of the devil (Juju) as well.

Juju means" Magic luck" - **Bad juju** "a superstitious belief in the karmic consequences of an action or behavior, usually negative in connotation". **Juju,** an object that has been deliberately infused with magical power, or the magical power itself. It also can refer to the belief system involving the use of **Juju**. Juju is practiced in West African countries such as Nigeria, Benin, Togo, and Ghana, although its assumptions are shared by most African people. It is neither good nor bad, but it may be used for constructive purposes, as well as for nefarious deeds.

A monkey's head is probably the most common **juju** in West Africa. The word **juju** is believed to be derived from the French joujou ("play thing"), though some sources claim(s) it is from the Hausa language, meaning **"fetish"** or **"evil spirit."**

It has been said that juju doesn't affect Americans, and those of us from the west just do not believe in it. What westerners do believe in is a bullet. If you shoot the leader of a juju group he will surely die. But just not believing in something will not always help you.

Leila Ali, former female boxing champion and daughter of Heavyweight Boxing legend Muhammad Ali, famously stated that *"just because you believe you are not afraid of your opponents, doesn't mean you not going to get your ass whooped"*.

Former heavyweight boxing champion Mike Tyson who's famous for first round knockouts stated: "**every** *fighter comes into the ring believing in his plan until he gets punched in the mouth"*.

During my construction projects for the Federal Government, we hired a white American former oil rig employee to head our equipment maintenance department. He was from Texas and his Nigerian girlfriend would always show up at the end of each month to collect his salary, and leave him almost nothing to make it to the next month. Everyone would plead with me to get Mr. Frank to return home. Even the US embassy would also assist him. He adamantly refused any thought of returning home because he appeared to be so in love with his girlfriend that he abandoned both his country and family.

As far as I know, even today seven years later he still resides in Delta State. I am not saying he believes in juju, nor am I saying he is under the influence of juju. But I find it very strange that one would abandon his former way of life in America, and family, to live in abject poverty in a third world country.

Although I don't believe in juju, I do believe and trust in the power of God. Moreover, as a result of my spiritual teaching from my mother, I pray daily and bless my living environment with incense while praying each morning. And I carry on with my day as if **juju** will never enter my spirit.

I would often wonder why, after the Europeans colonized almost 100% of the countries on the African continent, did they all of a sudden begin to leave starting with Ghana's Independence in 1957. Algeria is the exception because they fought bitterly prior to getting their independence. Surely it wasn't because they were defeated by war nor did they completely deplete the natural resources of the continent. Perhaps one of many factors could have been that the wives became annoyed and furious with their husbands not returning home.

I've learned that it is not uncommon to sit in a meeting or relax in an eatery with educated, well-traveled Nigerians, who would survey the environment and make statements like, "one must be aware as some of the people in this environment although walking, talking, eating and drinking are actually dead." It is also not uncommon to be cautioned by a fellow Nigerian that you should stay away from certain beautiful women as they may be from "mama water". By this they mean looking fresh as being newly reborn from the land of the deceased or a spiritual creature.

Additionally, it has been said that the Oshodi market has wicked people and witches. If one is bold enough to take the wax out of the corner of a dog's eye and place it in the corner of your own, look under the tables in the market, you may find that some of the workers are levitating above ground as they stand.

Nigeria at night is a very eerie place, especially in small towns and villages. You can have all the hustle and bustle similar to that of New York City just before and during rush hour and, two hours later(,) without the sound of generators, it will be so quiet that you will feel as if you're the last person on earth. I have come to learn that when relaxing or shopping in a crowded market place, if someone begins shouting "thief!, thief!," just stand proudly if you're sitting and begin looking left and right for the thief, but do not run. Running may cause you to be mistaken as the thief and you could be subjected to jungle justice, tried, and punished on the spot. And later the mob will be informed that you were to be the keynote speaker at tomorrow's convention.

Who Turned out the Lights?

In Nigeria, make an honest attempt to never travel alone. It is better to be like American rappers and travel with a crew. In the event of any accident or injury it is rare that a Nigerian will oblige to involve himself. Only those that know you will risk taking you to the hospital or to the police, as it could result in one being accused of causing the injury or death. And, if found guilty, you will suffer the consequences, especially in small towns or village's.

If your driver is moving at high speed either due to reckless driving or suspecting he is being pursued by potential criminals, and he happens to hit a pedestrian or okada (bike operator), it is wise not to stop. Just keep going until you reach a police station where you can report the incident, as stopping could be the death of your driver because everyone in the village is family.

Most Okada (motorized bikes) have been banned from major roads and cities however, should one need to catch a ride and if you have a choice, always ride on the bike of an older operator. It's safer and maybe he has a family and will be less reckless during your transport.

In Nigeria, most armed robberies don't just happen by chance. It's usually by information given to the criminals by any of the following persons that know your movements and financial assets: your personal driver, your house help, your cab man, your neighbor or even your banker. The request made by the criminals would be so informative that the Nigerian victim would think it must be juju, when in fact it is just information provided by someone you trusted.

Kindness, compassion and tipping, not necessarily in that order, is your greatest security in the country. When I first arrived, the average tip was about 20 naira. Today's average tip is between 100 and 200 naira or more depending on the quality of service rendered. It is very easy to tip your mechanic, security personnel, house help, tailor, store clerk, doorman, civil servants, police, etc. to show appreciation. The more people you show appreciation to, the safer you will become in Nigeria.

In America, police often get complimentary coffee, donuts, sometimes meals, and reduced apartment rental rates. However, they don't accept cash tips. I don't have a problem providing modest appreciation to Nigerian police or security personnel while in the line of duty. If you promise someone in Nigeria something and tell them you will get back in touch, after some time, they will attempt to get your attention by texting you one of the following: Happy Sunday, Happy New week, Happy Monday, Happy New Month, etc. My Nigerian host once asked me why the first thing Black Americans do is shout for their mothers when in trouble and I answered, "Maybe because Mother is our first Love". Weeks later I asked him what was the Nigerian infatuation with the cell phone and he stated *"because it's the only thing in the country that works"*.

The Nigerian Military, Police and most other security personnel in the country have a unique way of accessing you by sight. Oftentimes without you even speaking, they will notice your movement, clothes and how you wear them. They are always looking to notice a difference because Nigerians truly *know themselves*. In Nigeria, when meeting with someone and you are ready to go, you tell him *"I'm coming"*.

In Nigeria, constant lights are a major problem. When lights are restored, often your house boy will tell you *"light don come"*, and turn off your generator. When two Nigerians from Edo State are talking on the phone and you want to know the other person's location, you will ask "where you dey?" In Nigeria, the famous last words during a meeting with suspected 4-1-9 criminals is *"No Walhalla" (no problem)*.

If you ever travel to Pankshin or Langtang (LGA) in Plateau State, this is where Nigerians can find some of the sweetest *"dog meat pepper soup" in the country*. How does an American know the difference between bush meat and chicken? *When you spit out the buckshot pellet. A* Nigerian rabbit looks like an American *"rat."* I will never eat a Nigerian rabbit.

In Nigeria, domestic help will cheat you, but they will *"cheat you right"*. If you are a troublesome person then don't go to Minna in Niger state because the citizens are humble and kind, and they do not like trouble. If you bring trouble, they will chase you. There exist many laws in Nigeria, perhaps even more laws than in America however, (;) it's the enforcement of those laws which are the issues.

Nigeria is considered a free country and all Americans want freedom, but I don't believe Americans can really handle true freedom. In Nigeria, far too many citizens run traffic lights, drive without drivers' license, without working head and tail lights or brakes on their vehicles. Some Nigerians drive without knowing how to drive. They drive without insurance and they even drive the opposite way going down a one way street. They also drive on the sidewalk and some drive drunk. You can buy drugs, sell drugs and smoke weed. You can beat the hell out of the electric company personnel that comes to disconnect your power line and you can discipline your children.

Some citizen's get away with talking to police any kind of way. You can urinate in public, throw trash on the ground as you stand, lie, cheat, steal and, if good enough at it, one day become the leader of the Nigerian people, just to name a few offenses in the country. Additionally, you can be booked and go to jail for all the above but remember, the only real crime in Nigeria, *"is not having money"*.

Far too many Nigerians have questions of confidence when it comes to the police. They feel that they never respond to matters of urgency in a timely manner unless you know a police officer personally. It's difficult to get them to respond via a telephone call. I have been going to Nigeria for years and I have yet to get a number to call a police station or emergency service personnel. Primarily, the police will usually arrive only after the crime has been committed, and the criminals have departed the scene

.

Therefore, Nigerians that can afford it build tall block walls around their homes and businesses, with glass bits, barbed wire, or electric wire on top. They also cover all windows in the home with steel. Many even hire 24 hour armed security for their own personal safety. In defense of the Police, when questioned regarding the above you will hear the top three major complaints:

1. Our salary, weapons and equipment are not commensurate with the risk and demands of the job.

2. If killed in the line of duty, who will take care of my wife and children.

3. There is no fuel in the police vehicle, you must come to the station to file your complaint, and purchase fuel or provide transportation for us to come to the scene of the crime.

I have been told by a friend that, due to the lack of prompt actions by police, it leads many citizens to suspect that, when crimes are committed, the police may have prior knowledge of the crime. In some cases, they may even loan their weapons to criminals, or they are a part of the criminal gangs. I will not go so far as to claim such a profound statement against the Nigerian Police as being factual or true, because I have no evidence to prove such an allegation.

It is the common people's duty to police the police

- Steven Magee

Nigerian police motto "Police is your friend"

-THISDAY

While telling jokes, an American Southern gentleman asked me "By what name do you call a one legged dog?" I thought for a moment and said I don't know he replied *"nothing because he ain't gonna come no damn way".*

- American Southern Gentlemen

Who Turned out the Lights?

When traveling to Nigeria remember there are two legal systems, one for locals and another for foreigners. The law can be absorbed under certain conditions for residents but, in the case of foreigners, they must face the full wrath of justice.

-Lagos times

Who Turned out the Lights?

CHAPTER 5: THE COURAGE TO HOPE

N igeria is a very complex country. Its governance is complicated by tribal, religious and sectional rivalries. Compared to America, it is also a very young democratic country, having just received its independence from Britain in October 1, 1960. Additionally, the country became a democracy for a brief period from 1979 to 1983, and officially May 29, 1999.

The year was 2008. I received my first engineering contract to perform construction consulting and provide an erosion control plan for the project. The contract was with B. R. Construction Company Ltd., owned by my friend Chief Ralph. It was a road project in Owerri, Imo State, the heart of Igbo land; which suffered heavy bombing during the Nigerian civil war of 1967 to 1970.

I made so many visits to the continent of Africa between my second visit in 2001 and 2008, that I had to add additional pages to my international passport, even though two years remained(,) before its expiration date. During this time we visited community leaders, local government chairmen, and first class chiefs in four-star hotels to small village fifth class chiefs peddling bicycles. Additionally, this was the period I came to understand the power of tradition in Nigeria.

Who Turned out the Lights?

In many cases, African tradition is stronger than the law. One should never enter the home of a Chief empty handed so we made sure to provide our share of live goats, hot drinks (liquor) and cash at our most important meetings. We visited places like Ahoda and Ogoni in Rivers State, Ankpa, Idah and Okene in Kogi State, and Oguwachukwu and Bruutu in Delta State. We also visited Auchi in Edo State, Aba in Abia State, and Surulere and Mafoloku in Lagos State, just to name a few places.

After opening with a greeting to the Chief, you would present your gift. Then you would serve or be served a certain wine depending on where you were. In Igbo land it was "Bitter kola nut" or "Garden Egg", and in Yoruba land "Kola nut" or "Palm Wine." These were served as a blessed fruit to welcome special guests.

(Two thousand and Eight) 2008 was also the year America elected its first African American President, Barack Obama. Maybe President Donald Trump was privileged to a bit of African folklore when claiming Obama was not an American. As in the African tradition, you are a native of the land where your father was born. Barack Obama, Sr. was born June 18, 1936 in Nyagnoma Kogelo, Kenya. Therefore, according to African tradition, Barack Obama is a Kenyan.

Who Turned out the Lights?

As for me, my father was born in Gadsden, Alabama and my mother Augusta, Georgia so, according to African folklore, I am an American from Gadsden, Alabama USA.

After acquiring seven years of on ground knowledge, I realized that Nigeria can be a very precarious place due to lack of emergency services, prompt police response, and a lack of good roads and lighting. Yes, it has crime, corruption and daily power outages. Life in the Giant of Africa can be discouraging at best, but it is also a country of abundance and opportunities abound for business. The country has a highly educated population and a government struggling to find its way. Today, about half of Nigeria's population live in extreme poverty. An absolute number more than any other country in the world, according to former US Ambassador to Nigeria, John Campbell.

In spite of the poverty, Nigerian's are often considered high on the list of some of the world's happiest people. I see a vibrant energetic population, infused with a unique and steadfast hope for a brighter future whether it's through politics, education, starting a business, ministerial service or traveling abroad to work in another country. Nigerians are filled with the "courage to hope". I see too many talented Nigerian's shackled to the actions of a struggling Democracy. One can only experience the true depth of their despair by going deep inside the country to meet the common Nigerian. The common man will communicate where he is if you listen attentively when he talks about his hopes, dreams and aspiration for his future. Maybe through my writing others can now hear the cries from those struggling on Salami Street in Lagos, upper third   junction in Benin City, Aba road in Port Harcourt, Minna in Niger State and Lugbe Street in Abuja.

"Like a tree falling in the forest that no one hears" is the statement made by President Jonathan prior to conceding defeat in the 2015 election. *The blood of not one Nigerian is worth more than his political ambition."* Only history will prove how profound a statement of change it was. It is therefore our hope that other African politicians and Godfathers will embrace his lead and bring about a new African political mind set.

I can see change coming to Nigeria as there used to be trash lining the streets of Lagos everywhere, now there is trash in Lagos somewhere. There used to be death traps called Okada on the roads everywhere, now Okada's are only on the roads somewhere. Outside of Abuja and other major cities there used to be very few high standard roads anywhere, now there are high standard roads somewhere. There used to be no reasonable way to make an international call anywhere, now you can make an inexpensive international call everywhere.

You used to have to carry cash in a suitcase everywhere, now, unless headed to your bank, there is no need to carry a suitcase of cash anywhere. You used to only be able to go on the Internet somewhere, now you can go online anywhere. You used to see heavy smoke coming from trucks on the road everywhere, now you only see heavy smoke remitting trucks somewhere. You used to see reckless drivers everywhere, now you only see reckless drivers somewhere. You used to be harassed for tips at the international airport by staff everywhere, now there's only modest harassment at the airport somewhere.

You used to see Nigerians robbed and thrown out of fast moving one-chance buses in Lagos everywhere, now people are only robbed in one-chance transport buses somewhere. You used to hear of police killing innocent Nigerians by way of accidental discharge of their weapons everywhere, now accidental discharge of a policeman's weapon only occurs somewhere.

On the flip side, you used to see potholes in roads everywhere, today you still see potholes in roads everywhere. You used to see and hear the smoke and noise of generators everywhere, you still see smoke and noise from generators everywhere. You used to have power outages everywhere, today you still have power outages everywhere.

You used to have armed robbery and kidnapping in Nigeria everywhere, you still have out of control kidnapping and robbery everywhere. Nigerians believe in and utilize the power of juju everywhere today; It is still widely practiced in Nigeria everywhere. By the grace of Allah and the "courage to hope", positive and enduring change is coming. When change comes to the Giant of Africa it's a process for change that will affect all of Africa. Today upon entering the country through the new Nnamdi Azikiwe international Airport, the first thing you will notice is that the new Abuja airport is modern, exceptionally bright, clean and functioning properly.

Many Nigerians will be quick to comment that it was the handwork of the former President Goodluck Jonathan, which is true. However, in my humble opinion, it is equally important to praise President Buhari for his efforts to insure that the project was completed for the Nigerian citizenry, as a symbol of pride and a bold and positive step forward for a new political mindset of cooperation and continuation.

Who Turned out the Lights?

"We all do better when we work together. Our differences do matter, but our common humanity matters more".

-

Bill Clinton

Who Turned out the Lights?

CHAPTER 6: CHOCOLATE CITY

The year was 2009. It would be my second project located in the City of Lagos, capital of Lagos State. The area was called Oshodi-Isolo LGA or Mafoloku. The scope of work was a one kilometer road paving project with drainage to be constructed deep in the heart of Oshodi on Salami Street.

For most Americans, Mafoloku is a place you would never visit unless you had family or business there. It is not a great vacation destination. It would be like having the third ward neighborhood in Houston, Texas, West Chicago, and Livernois Avenue, Mack Avenue and Helen Street areas in Detroit. Along with Liberty City and Overtown in Miami, The Fashion District and Watts in Los Angeles, Bed Sty and Crown Heights in Brooklyn, New York and Bankhead Highway area in Atlanta, all rolled into one...a real "chocolate city".

It was because of my Nigerian host connection with the local Oshodi Chairman that our group received the project. Lagos was listed to have a population of around 18 million. A local newspaper informed the locals that a special count was performed by the State government and, due to the high homeless rate, the study did not count individuals. Instead, they counted dwellings, homes, apartments or any structure where locals slept. The count was around 9 million dwellings and the average household in Lagos had three to six people. Considering three people per dwelling, that gives us an estimated population count of 27 million people. It appeared that at least five thousand of them lived on Salami Street alone.

There was also one other significant factor about Oshodi, the rich and middle class. In order to leave the country or city by air one must pass through Oshodi, as it is home to the Muhammad International and Lagos Domestic Airports. As an American coming to perform road construction in a mega city like Lagos, you will need to adjust your mindset to allow the people to truly become a part of your work. They will drive and walk all over your work, and even throw trash daily.

Also, on newly excavated road way work, they will eat and cook in the roadway. They will park and remove any temporary barricade they can after close of work. Sometimes, they will be inches away from the swing of your hammer, the spin of your saw blade or tires of your heavy equipment while in operation. As the local street chairman stated during our weekly meetings, his people are a bit uncultivated (village people).

There was even a home constructed at the end of the road. The home was in the middle of the street based on the proposed road design. Therefore, it was scheduled to be removed because the home was rumored to be inhabited by a local Oshodi juju woman. Therefore, being an American, I was charged with the responsibility of removing the structure, and was provided with red paint and a brush by the Local government, to notify the occupants of the home that it would soon be demolished.

As previously mentioned, I respect the country's tradition but for me, stated before, I do not believe in juju. I believe in the power of God. The next day, I marked the house with a large red painted X–OILG and demolished it three months later. Thereafter, the Nigerian workers would caution me that a juju edifice was being placed on the jobsite, and pointed out its location each morning as a new edifice of some kind would be placed there. I would just pray, calmly kick it into the ditch and walk away. I commenced my day's work. The job was filled with all types of unusual challenges but I never attributed any of them to juju.

Prior to me coming to site, there was a new drainage structure on both sides of the street being constructed by another Nigerian contractor. The water was so contaminated that only a local could dare allow himself to be emerged in it, even wearing knee high rubber boots. Surprisingly, the boys removed their shoes and worked in a water filled ditch with all sorts of rubbish, including but not limited to, urine.

During the project I had never set eyes on a Nigerian mosquito, as they only bit me on the back of my arms, ankles or elbows, or at night when there were no lights. Mosquitos were everywhere, but I didn't see them. I was bitten so many times that the local inspector's first question was always "what happened to your arms?" Every Nigerian that I have ever employed at some point has taken ill to mosquito bites, causing typhoid or malaria. I thank God for providing me with good health. Because I take natural herbs provided by my mother I have never been ill since traveling to the continent of Africa. Moreover, I never drank tap or sachet water (bag water), only bottled water.

As an American, I would often wonder why every morning Nigerians would greet you good morning and then add "how was your night?" This is usually never a question in America. After arriving at daybreak, our first order of business was to remove trash from the roadway on the jobsite. In the trash was always five to ten dead rats; They never tossed them in the ditches, I could only imagine the harrowing battles taking place throughout the night with marauding rats. Many of the workers would sleep on floors. The heat is overbearing with no electricity or light.

The rats would search for food among the sleeping, especially children. Rumors had it that they would even nibble and chew the hard skin on the bottoms of people's feet while they slept. Some people awake in the morning in excruciating pain from the rodent activities during the night. With this rumored knowledge, I now greet Nigerian's good morning then I ask, "How was your night?", as they typically reply "We thank God".

With thanks to the Chairman, I was provided a hotel room and a three meals per day credit by a supporter of the Chairman. The name of the hotel was B-Jay in Oshodi, not in Victoria Island. It was one of the most relaxing places. Most of the heads of state and local politicians would often come to drink, eat and relax there. It was because of my friendship with the local heads of the politicians, Iron lady (head female representative) and the area boys (gang members), that I was able to move around Oshodi safely. Along with the fact that I was upgrading the community by providing a new tarred road.

One evening during a courtesy visit to my hotel by the Honorable Chairman, there was the sound of gunfire outside the hotel. As guests began to seek cover by returning to their rooms, I noticed that the Chairman's personal police officer had removed his shirt, allowing his tee shirt to cover his pistol. I had never seen such a Lily-livered act by a police officer, but oftentimes methods of survival in Nigeria makes it a uniquely different kind of place. It was later confirmed that the policeman had a wife and children.

Who Turned out the Lights?

One Friday evening after work, I was summoned by the Honorable Chairman's security police to attend a political fundraiser in his honor. Upon arrival, I was seated next to the Chairman in the VIP section with all the financial donors and heads of the Oshodi local government. The dinner consisted of rice, bush meat and all you could drink. After some time, I asked the chairman to excuse me because I was about retiring for the night. He suggested I stay at the hotel, but I felt the need to return to my hotel at B-Jay's after some discussion.

I was kindly provided a ride back to my hotel by one of the leaders of the area boys group, and his second in command. Oshodi is a local government area of Lagos with over one million residents. It is considered a slum area, although it contains the Lagos domestic and International Airport. At night it is dark, deathly silent, and frightening. While en route, we noticed flickering of flashlights in the center of the road.

It quickly became apparent it was a Nigerian police checkpoint, although less than ten feet on either side of the road were makeshift shacks or homes inhabited by hundreds of Nigerians. But it was so silent that it felt no different than being pulled over on a lonely country road in south Alabama, Georgia or Mississippi... but this was the Lagos "chocolate city" center.

Who Turned out the Lights?

This was not a stop for *appreciation* (tips) or small talk, the sound of gunfire would not engender this group to remove their shirts. This was attentive, observant, and deliberate police business. The Police checked vehicle particulars and searched for drugs and weapons. The lead officer spoke clearly and moved with caution. Even in the darkness, I could feel from my peripheral vision that the car was surrounded. The officer gave clear instructions and the driver obeyed without question. I remained motionless and quiet in the rear seat. I was also praying that they would not ask us to come down, as I knew police are not interested in taking you to be booked back at the station. In Nigeria, trial and punishment are often discerned on the spot.

I prayed that this incident would not be the end of the road for me. Furthermore, should anything deadly happen here, my family would never know how much of an innocent victim I absolutely was. The entire episode felt like a movie in slow motion and it was never ending. Somehow without noticing, the police accessed every occupant in the vehicle. Typically they will have no business with anyone except the driver so you should remain quiet and non-combative.

By way of a silent act of mutual respect, professional Nigerian police will not disturb passengers. Thankfully, and finally after a thorough inspection of the vehicles particular and the boot (trunk), we were allowed to proceed. The leader of the area boys praised the police for their professional work as we slowly and cautiously drove away. That particular night, I learned there are perhaps ninety-nine safe places to be out at night in Lagos, but Oshodi wasn't one.

Thereafter, I remained focused on the task at hand, which was the successful completion of the project. As an American and an ambassador of goodwill, it was incumbent of me to carry myself as a professional with integrity, generosity, and to demonstrate goodwill in all that I did. Often I would feed the children, as long as the parents never knew I was the source of payment. I provided jobs to youth and tasked them in cleaning the roadway of trash and debris every day, even when I returned to America on break. We worked with the area boys (local gangs) and provided employment through political favors. The Honorable Chairman was gracious enough to provide credit for us to rent heavy equipment from local government contacts. Since time was always of the essence, I would use my own money to assist in funding the project.

My Nigerian partner rarely visited the project, but when it was near the final stage of completion (placing the asphalt), he visited the site to make a payment to the asphalt contractor. During this visit, he felt the need to read me the riot act in the presence of the site officials and the subcontractors. Although I worked with everyone daily, I also informed everyone that my partner was the boss of the project. Therefore, his word and decisions were final.

This was the second time in my life that I felt like going postal but I humbled myself, held my peace, and remained on ground working throughout the Christmas season. I completed the job. To add financial insult, my partner paid me a contemptible 2.5 million naira ($16,000 USD) and, from that amount, I had to reimburse the hotel for food. At the end of the day, it was very close to the amount of money that I used to fund the job.

The community leaders, salami street residents and sub-contractors were not happy, and even utterly surprised, when they found out about my compensation. They were also expecting appreciation from me at the end of the project. Although highly disappointed, I voiced my disgust to my partner verbally and in writing and let the matter take its course. I have never, just let it go.

In Nigeria, I learned sometimes you meet crime, corruption, deceit, trickery and what is termed the "Nigerian Contest". In my humble opinion this means, when engaged in business with a Nigerian, if he or she "wants to be fast", lies, cheats, scams and fools you to his or her advantage, than it is not truly a crime or a lie in their eyes. They feel like they outsmarted you and got away.

Who Turned out the Lights?

Recognizing the shared experience will help foreigners better understand cab drivers and other merchants in Nigeria. Good honest business takes place in Nigeria everywhere. Similarly, the "Nigerian Contest" takes place everywhere as well. Our Company returned to Lagos three years later to perform maintenance on the Salami street road project with the consent of the current local government chairman.

It has been said, there is only one caveat regarding Nigeria: come with your eyes wide open and with an intelligence radar that is at par with that of your hosts. The country has a thriving workforce and labor, exceptionally brilliant individuals and unmatched business acumen across the continent.

Lagos times

CHAPTER 7: ANCIENT CITY OF BENIN

Benin City, capital of Edo State Nigeria, has a long history of civilization. Historians and researchers trace its existence as far back as prehistoric time. As Prince E. Eweka put it, "No one is really certain about the origin of the Edo people, whose origin appears to have been lost in myths and legends of the distant past".

What is very certain is that Edo Civilization is well over 6000 years, according to scientific evidence. The Portuguese visited Benin City around 1485. Benin grew rich during the 16th and 17th Centuries, mostly through trade with slaves, pepper and Ivory. A Portuguese captain described the city in 1691; "Great Benin", where the King resides, is larger than Lisbon. All the streets run straight and as far as the eye can see. The houses are large, especially that of the King, which is richly decorated and has fine columns. The city is wealthy and industrious. It is also so well governed that theft is unknown, and the people live in such security that they have no doors to their houses". This was at a time when theft and murder was rife in London.

Eweka I and the beginning of the Oba era. (About 1200 AD-1235 AD).

Who Turned out the Lights?

For a period of over 30 years, the administration of Benin City was virtually in the hands of the Ogiamien family. Until 1200 AD when the "Boy King" Eweka, a young King, ruled the kingdom with the assistance of his maternal grandfather Ogiegor. Oba Eweka I, started the reign of Obas. Hitherto, the kings were known as Ogiso but when Eweka I came as King, he was referred to as Oba. Some people said that the word Oba is a Yoruba word which means King. Others said the word Oba meaning is hard or difficult, probably from an abbreviation of the original name of the first Ogiso {Obagodo {Oba godo) - Oba King; godo-high: High King). Wherever the word is derived from, one can say that it really came into use as connoting Kingship during Oba Eweka I in 1200 AD. Oba Eweka I reined for 35 years at his demise. His rival children ruled in succession.

Prince Idugbowa was the eldest son of Oba Adolo and his mother was called queen Iheya. During his coronation, he took the name Oba Ovonramwen Nogbaisi in 1888. He was tall, charismatic, very bold and possessed a majestic voice. He was blessed with children: Prince Aiguobasimwin, Usuanlele, Ehigie and Uvbi princesses: Evbakhavbokun, Omono, and Orimwiame. May 1891, during the royal coral beads ceremony, a human sacrifice was offered to the Gods. His name was Thomas Oyibodudu. During his execution he shouted saying, "The white men that are greater than us are

coming shortly to conquer you and I, but do it quickly."
True to his words, the prophecy manifested in 1897.

In 1853, the British made contact with the Binis to
trade pepper, palm oil, clothes and Ivory. Due to its
economic and military power, Benin independently ran
its trading activities in its region and was not subjected to
orders from any other kingdom or empire, not even
Britain. The British found this displeasing and inimical.
Their lifetime mission was to annex Benin into the
British Empire and depose the King, Oba Ovonramwen
Nogbaisi, if necessary.

In 1892, Henry Gallway, a British Vice –Consul,
visited Benin with the intention of annexing the kingdom
through a treaty. He presented the so-called treaty of
"trade and friendship" to the Oba who was skeptical
about it, and Britain as well. Oba Ovonramwen however,
signed the treaty agreeing to stop slavery and human
sacrifice in Benin. But later, when Oba Ovonramwen
realized that the treaty was nothing but a tactic to annex
Benin into the British Empire, he forbade his people to
trade with the British, and barred the white men from
entering Benin. The British saw this as a violation of the
1892 treaty, and thus bent on punishing the Oba.

A British invasion force headed by Phillips set out
to overthrow the Oba in 1896. Phillips sent a request to
the British authorities in London for permission to invade
Benin and depose the Oba. Without waiting for approval,

Who Turned out the Lights?

Phillips set out for Benin with "friendly troops". The friendly troops consisted of two trading agents, two Niger coast protectorate officers, a medical officer and 250 African soldiers in the guise as porters.

The force's weapons were hidden in baggage. Phillips' plan was to gain access to Oba Ovonramwen's palace by announcing that he intended to negotiate. Ovonramwen's messengers issued several warnings not to violate Benin territorial sovereignty, claiming he was unable to see Phillips due to ceremonial duties. Having been warned on several further occasions on the way, Phillips sent his stick to the Oba. This was a deliberate insult designed to provoke the conflict that would provide the excuse for British annexation. Phillips' expedition was ambushed and all but two were killed. The event was known as the "Benin Massacre".

On hearing the news of Phillips death, the British authorities decided to punish Benin. Thus, on the 12th of July 1897, Rear Admiral Harry Rawson (the British commander and chief at Cape Town) was appointed to lead the invasion of Benin kingdom and capture Oba Ovonramwen. The operation was called the "Benin Punitive Expedition". It was known in Nigerian history as "Benin expedition of 1897" or "Benin Invasion of 1897".

The bombardment of Benin began on the 9th of February in 1897. Benin forces tried to repel the attack but their weapons, which mainly consisted of machetes, spears and arrows, were no match for the British sophisticated rifles and cannons. All houses in the kingdom were torched. The people were killed irrespective of their gender, age or status. An order was given to hang   Oba Ovonramwen whenever and wherever he was found. British troops were about 1,200 heavily armed, and mostly African. The African fraction of the British troops did most of the fighting, while the British soldiers sat behind machine guns and cannons.

It is worthy of note that Benin Kingdom had existed from time immemorial, and had thrived extensively as one of the most prosperous and mightiest kingdoms in West Africa during the 15th and 16th century. When Benin City was invaded and eventually fell to the British forces in 1897, Edo land was placed under the jurisdiction of the southern protectorate. The fall of the Benin Empire was an event the British colonial power has always hoped for. It gave them the opportunity to stretch their Empire to the West Africa hinterland. With the Benin Empire out of the way, a country called *Nigeria* was born.

The Oba was captured before British law was found guilty, deposed and exiled with two of his wives in Calabar where he died in 1914. After Ovonramwen's passing, his son, Prince *Aiguobasimwin*, was enthroned as the Oba on the 24th of July in 1914. (, taking) He then took the name Eweka II after the 13th-century founder of the dynasty, Eweka I.

On September 5, 2011, I entered the *Ancient City of Benin* for the first time to commence work on a new Aviation Hanger 2-Story Office Building and Workshop for the Federal Government. We traveled from Abuja and approached the City by private jet, flying near the Oba's palace, and landing at the Benin City Airport. After being received by the Nigerian Air force commander, our team was shown to its new residence located at Number Twenty Seven B *Aiguobasimwin* Crescent Benin City, Edo State - Nigeria.

Who Turned out the Lights?

References:

Thomas Uwadiale Obinyan the Annexation of Benin

Sven Lindqvist Exterminate All the Brutes

Oba of Benin Archived at the Way back machine

Edo Historical Traditional Cultural Heritage

Toyin Falola Pre-colonial Nigeria

Bondarenko D.M. Benin Kingdom of the 13th to 19th Centuries

Wikipedia

"How can you have a war on terrorism when war itself is terrorism?"

-

Howar d Zinn

Who Turned out the Lights?

CHAPTER 8: DUBIOUS DISTINCTION

One day I was having a casual conversation with a friend who is a Native born Nigerian, an Aircraft Pilot, who traveled the world extensively and was educated in Nigeria, England and America. During our conversation he stated, "I could never see myself living in any country other than my beloved Nigeria".

In-spite of the negative attitude and propaganda by the world press against the continent of Africa, Nigeria in particular, it is not the worst, nor most corrupt place in the world. Most of its citizens are unaware of its country's dubious distinction until they travel abroad. Nigeria has a higher GDP than Norway and the United Arab Emirates. Poverty is not due to lack of wealth, but the failure to distribute the wealth evenly. Additionally, according to a Citigroup report published in February 2011, Nigeria will have the world's highest average GDP growth in the world between 2010 and 2050. Nigeria will also become the third largest country by 2050.

Additionally, Nollywood, the Nigerian movie industry, is fastly becoming the top industry in the world. I see a country that has a University system which produces millions of smart aggressive graduates every year, but with no real job opportunities. There are only so many government positions but they go to the most connected applicants only. Therefore, you have a highly educated employable workforce of about 20 million unemployed, poised to be given an opportunity to exercise their skills. This lack of opportunities is the main and simple reason why you will find taxi drivers with Business, Engineering, Internet Technology and Law degrees.

You will find hotel receptionists with Nursing, Accounting and Teaching degrees. You will also find domestic servants skilled in carpentry, electrical, construction and plumbing trades. The country is creating two types of citizens outside of the already rich and established business group. Those who are law abiding that exercise patience and have the "courage to hope", and those who are fed up with waiting on leadership and want fast change.

A fortunate few travel abroad, only if well connected. Others risk their lives by traveling based on false promises of jobs that do not exist. Additionally, a subsection of this group may also engage in criminal activities whether in politics, drug dealing, robbery, or kidnapping, which occurs in every country. It is the crimes of advance fee fraud, confidence tricks or 4-1-9 scams, carried out mostly by young, male and educated ("Yahoo Boys"), which gives Nigeria the notorious reputation of being a land soiled with criminality. But in reality it's because this particular group of internet fraudsters are so "damn clever". The use of computer charm, a universal recognizable crime instrumental in creating the "dubious distinction", is something that the country carries throughout the world.

Nigerian children are only one year, six months, four days, six minutes and a dirty slap away for being responsible enough to look out for themselves.

-Loving Nigerian parent

One Birth every 4 seconds

    One Death every 14 seconds

    One net migrant every nine minutes

    Net gain one person every 6 seconds

    -Nigerian population in 2018 Source: By Supashegs Olusegun Adrinto

"How do you convince the upcoming generations that education is the key to success when we are surrounded by poor graduates and rich criminals?"

- Robert Mugabe

"The will to survive is a want"

Goodwill Ambassador Al McAfee, Jr.

Who Turned out the Lights?

CHAPTER 9: FIRM FOUNDATION

O ur third contract in Nigeria was to construct an Aviation Hangar Two-Story Office Building. Also, to construct a workshop for the Presidential Implementation Committee on Maritime Safety and Security (PICOMSS), which would later be taken over by the Nigerian Air Force in Benin City. The client required all design drawings and materials to be shipped from America, with the exception of the concrete and reinforcing steel materials. Our firm, McAfee Design & Distributing Co. Inc., is an American Engineering and Construction company located in Atlanta, Georgia USA.

Additionally, we are recipients of the 1997 National Minority Construction firm of the year award, as well as many other awards. However, we are most proud of having the opportunity to provide jobs for all Americans, especially during times when very few job opportunities for minorities and disadvantaged citizens were available. We hired Blacks, Whites, Hispanic, Women, members of the LGTB community, the handicap, convicted felons looking for a fresh start, and veterans of foreign wars.

Who Turned out the Lights?

We realized that it is because of our sacrifices to exist as a business that we have made our City, State and Country a better, safer and more prosperous society. Moreover, we felt delighted and grateful to be given such an esteemed opportunity to provide employment and training to citizens of the Giant of Africa (Nigeria).

For the work on this project the client provided an enabling environment, namely mobilization. We rented a five-bedroom home with a laundry room, boy's quarters, a house boy, gardener, two gatemen, a personal driver, and two armed 24 hour security personnel in a secure compound with eight foot high block walls with barbed wire atop. We also purchased a pickup truck and Ford SUV Jeep.

The compound had its own water supply and a 100K diesel generator to insure 24 hour power supply when needed. The project would be our most challenging to date. It included all the elements of international business: high seas international shipping, port acquisition of imported goods from a foreign country and the overland transport of 26 containers from Lagos Tin Can Port to Benin City. We were tasked to complete the Construction of an Aviation Hanger large enough to house two large Aircraft, a two story office building, a workshop and drainage.

Who Turned out the Lights?

The project also consisted of the construction of a box covered bridge carrying the weight of large aircraft, along with concrete construction, reinforcing steel installation, structural steel installation, plumbing, electrical and mechanical. Lastly, we were also responsible for hauling sand gravel and suitable soil to the site, building a concrete access road, an asphalt taxiway, interior dry walling, tiling, painting and furnishing. Our most important responsibility was a hiring a workforce that had minimal experience working with American materials and tools.

As the work commenced, I did not feel the Air force Commander was an initial advocate of the project taking place adjacent to his base. He questioned my expertise and ability to complete such a large technical project. Although he was the first person I met upon arrival to Benin, I do recall that he was in civilian clothes during our initial meeting without the owner of the project present. The commander was not sure we had previously met.

Our first on site meeting consisted of the Commander arriving at the site and summoning me from my work. I was surrounded by his security detail. It was not an aggressive action and I never felt threatened, it was just the manner in which the Commander of the esteemed Nigerian Air force rolled. I was in fact impressed by the manner in which the Air force group moved in precise formation; they were tall, immaculately outfitted, alert and fit for duty.

As the Commander introduced himself and began to question me regarding the scope of work taking place, I did my best to brief him. There was very little small talk and, minutes later, he and his detail departed. Several weeks later the commander called me once again, this time to report to his office in the presence of his ranking officers. The request was made that we move the entire structure from its current design location an additional 25 meters into the bush, after over 30 minutes of discussion regarding changing the location.

I humbled myself because one mistake one should never make, is to show disrespect to an Air force General, especially in a foreign country. I calmly addressed each question remaining steadfast against change, while technically and methodically explaining the adverse effect moving the structure would create. Respecting the intelligence of the commander, it became apparent that if I could not defend the technical aspects and merits of the project, then surely I was not fit to construct it. After further discussion, the meeting concluded and we were allowed to commence work on the project in its original design location.

Who Turned out the Lights?

Compounding our problems, the American Supervisory team, who was contracted to complete the office building from Texas, departed the project without completing its consulting agreement. They claimed that the Nigerian workforce was unqualified and that I did not provide enough skilled labor. Additionally, the Hanger material supplier consulting team from Maine completed their consulting agreement. But they were so late arriving to Nigeria, that we already constructed 70% of the hanger's steel trusses and fabric before their arrival. Moreover, in Benin City it rained almost every day.

McAfee Design is an American firm. Our history comes from working with the US Banking Industry, the Private Sector and the State and Federal Department of Transportation. We refer to the latter group as "*the Good Old Boy Network*", although it is considered an unofficial catch phrase. The group with whom we worked to maintain control over the contracting dollars, consisted of some good old boys who paid you for the quality of your work, even though deep rooted historical attitudes were also working against us.

So, at the end of the day, this struggle became our strength. We countered our problems in Benin City by bringing in our Superintendent from the Atlanta office to complete the office building, and hang structural steel for the hanger. We hired a local quantity surveyor, two budding engineering grads from the local Nigerian University System, and the surveying company from our Lagos project. We hired a team of Muslims to manually construct our drainage system. The "Supervision" now **strapped up** and got into the hole, we now began demonstrating to the workers how rodbusters use pliers and reel to tie rebar quicker.   We tied two typical beams as an example.

The concrete finishers quickly came on line after we removed their first pour due to quality control. A few months later, we had sixty employees, mainly Nigerians. A highly skilled workforce, every man mastered his job quickly, as if it would be the last employment he would ever get. We paid a good wage and provided worker's compensation insurance.   We hired Blacks, Whites, Muslims, Christians and women. We also hired recent graduates, the young and the old, and the handicapped.

We worked in over 100 degree heat, and we worked weekends, (we worked at) nights and   even during the day in the rain. We also worked at night in the rain. I was often the last to leave the job and I reported to work every day. I did every job that I asked my workers to do except go up on the man-lift to hang steel. The Nigerian workforce was hard working, damn dependable, quick to learn new skills, cunning and clever. I was both cautious and impressed and had to manage sometimes with strength and energy, but mainly with fairness and logic.

On the surface, the boys will appear so genteel and humble, and their words would sound so sweet that you would believe their lips were laced with honey. But to lead them without losing your shirt, you must dissect the flesh and get to their core. Benin's have been recipients of cultural wisdom that goes as far back as prehistoric time. Consequently, you must get to the spirit of the person, as many in the group carry questionable character. Therefore, leading them was complicated and exhausting. It took every bit of God's blessings and my childhood teachings. With my American city street smarts and an HBCU and Ivy League education, the battles to survive the good old boy network and the project in Lagos strengthened my ability to lead and stay one step ahead of the group.

On May 16, 2013 during a stoppage of work, our structural steel foreman was shouting instructions to move our asphalt machine to another location to be repaired. It was to be moved for that repair process. He was shouting orders from inside the cage of our fully extended 60' man lift, which was used to assist the Crane in placing the steel trusses in the roof section of the aircraft hanger. He was alone in the bucket at the time wearing a full body harness, but he was not tied off as instructed during weekly safety meetings.

While shouting instructions and operating the control panel simultaneously, he accidentally engaged the hydraulic lift, and it penned his body between the structural steel and the equipment bucket. Upon witnessing what happened from the hanger floor 60' below, two of his colleagues rushed to his aid. They feverishly removed one of the bolted trusses to relieve the hydraulic pressure and Mr. Steven's body just collapsed into the bucket. He continued falling outside the bucket before rescue teams could react, dropping head first toward the concrete floor below. I saw him falling and immediately looked away, as I did   not want to see a direct impact with the concrete floor below.

All of the Nigerian eyewitnesses said it was as if a strong wind or the hand of God reached out and flipped his body around, causing him to land on his back. Additionally, eye witnesses stated that the 10" reinforced concrete floor appeared to turn into a soft mesh, as the body bounced up about six feet in the air after the initial impact. There was not one trace of blood anywhere.

I was infuriated that the rescue team allowed him to fall as every worker rushed to his aid. Thank God he had a pulse and was still breathing. We rushed him to the closest local hospital where emergency care was provided, but we were told he must be transferred to the University of Benin Teaching hospital due to the severity of his injuries. After composing myself and getting an injury report, I held a site meeting to ask everyone to pray, provided an update on Mr. Stevens' medical condition and retired to my office to begin writing the incident report. I also contacted the insurance company, project owner and my family.

After releasing the incident report, the chairman dispatched an aircraft to Benin because Mr. Stevens's condition could only be addressed at the specialist hospital in Ibadan. We assisted in removing several seats in the back of the aircraft to allow Mr. Stevens to enter the plane while still on the stretcher. My assistant accompanied Mr. Stevens along with his brother on the flight, and the two remained with him until his operation was completed. The insurance company required an incident and police report prior to any compensation, so I went to the Nigerian police station at the airport to report the incident. To our surprise, the Divisional Police Officer (DPO) of the station requested an unreasonable fee for the report.

It was because we were accompanied by an Air force officer that the matter was reported back to the commander. Days later, I was asked to report to the Air force office where the commander and several Nigerian Air Force (NAF) officers, along with the DPO of police were present. The Commander used such language in the meeting to make it abundantly clear to the DPO that the Air force and Police must work together. The Commander also told the DPO of Police that he should demonstrate his commitment to his duty by providing the requested report without conditions. The DPO then verbally stated that he would provide the report and the commander left the room. The DPO quickly rose up from his chair, stumped to his feet, looked me in the eyes and said "my father is from the water so beware." The following day our report was provided and, days later, the DPO was transferred and I never saw him again.

Due to the urgency of Mr. Stevens's health, the operation needed to be performed quickly, so the company paid a deposit as a partial payment for the operation. Mr. Steven broke several bones throughout his body but the spinal injury was the biggest concern. After some hours in the operating room, I was informed that the operation was successful. Mr. Steven survived but would never walk again because his spinal cord was injured beyond surgical repair. Two weeks later, he was released from the hospital, and returned back to his village in Delta State.

Who Turned out the Lights?

The insurance payment took several months to clear discretion. During this time we were hearing of disappointment from the village about the incident. I felt that the company had gone over and beyond the call of duty to save the life of one of its employees. A short time later, I was summoned to the Insurance Company to discuss reimbursement. After my meeting with the insurance executives, I was greeted in the office foyer by Mr. Stevens in a wheelchair, along with a group of elderly women from his village. They began by greeting me and making a   statement of hardship. Then they fell to the floor praying and crying in a language unknown. I felt distressed and disgruntled but I would not shed a tear until after hearing them out.

I quietly told them *"I'm coming"*. Thirty days later, I picked up the payment, drafted a not-to-sue settlement agreement to protect all parties involved through my Attorney, and I paid the majority of the compensation received from the Insurance settlement to Mr. Stevens.

On   January 29, 2015, the NAF released a PIMT Final Job Completion Certificate for Construction of the Aviation Hangar, which was built by McAfee Design & Distributing Co., Inc., located at 81 AMG Benin City. As a closely held African American owned business receiving no financial support from our government and having no financial partners, it is our hope that, through our initial struggles and successes, we can begin the process of establishing a firm foundation for generations of African Americans and other businesses to come.

Additionally, we would like to express our appreciation to the Nigerian Government, the Honorable Chairman, his Attorney (Bannister), and the Distinguished Captain that empowered us with the opportunity to prove the depth of our technical abilities and corporate mantle.

"In America you can buy one and get one free"

"In Nigeria you buy one and get none free"

- Goodwill Ambassador Al McAfee, Jr.

"A seasoned international businessman does not start, nor engage, in public conversation regarding rumors, lies or the truth about host countries governments; but it behooves him to listen."

- Goodwill Ambassador Al McAfee, Jr.

"In Nigeria, you have to know when to be an American and when to be quiet."

- Goodwill Ambassador Al McAfee, Jr.

Who Turned out the Lights?

"To a man with a hammer, every problem is a nail".

-Quote from movie death on the Orient express

Who Turned out the Lights?

CHAPTER 10: THE RICH

Forget the Brits and the Civets. Mexico, Indonesia, Nigeria and Turkey are the new kids on the block. According to economists, the wealth of the five richest men in Nigeria could end extreme poverty in the country. Public office holders stole an estimate $20 Trillion from the Treasury between 1960 and 2005.

Publicado 17 May 2017

There is an old saying in Nigeria that goes, *"if you ever want to get rid of a friend, just help him to get elected to Political office. Once on seat, he will never call you, allow you to visit him nor pick up your calls"*. During a church sermon in Benin City a pastor said "Nigerians are not wicked people, but they must stop stealing". Most Nigerians realize the great wealth possessed by the country and they pray passionately to acquire monetary favor from GOD. During a speech in London on leadership and wealth, American mega church Bishop TD Jakes commented that "prayer is not leadership, and not enough to make anyone rich. If prayer was enough   Nigeria would be the richest country in the world."

The rich or elite class of Nigerians are just ordinary people looked upon with an almost God like appraisal by the common Nigerian citizen. Not to be fooled, the rich do know that it is the money, not the person that is truly being praised. When the rich travel to America much of the music stops as Americans don't care about your political affiliation, or how much money you have, as long as you are spending and you wait *your turn in line.* **It is easier to meet an American President in office than to meet a sitting Governor in Nigeria.**

If you are not well connected, it is next to impossible to get a meeting with the President of Nigeria. The wealth that the rich have amassed through political office is unbelievable. It is difficult for me to wrap my head around how politicians and political appointees can acquire $100 million dollars or more on fixed salaries. It is therefore necessary for them to hide money, not just somewhere, but everywhere. They hide money in banks and investment in real estate, especially hotels, both foreign and domestic. They hide money in their homes, in the village and in the names of family members. They sleep on the money, they bury it and, when in doubt of a change in government, they move funds around in personally protected armored vehicles.

My rich friends and associates are former Presidents, Governors, Military Generals, Local Government Chairmen's, Bankers, Esteemed Religious men and women, Businessmen and Village Chiefs. They own private jets or have access to private aircraft. They own gold and coal mines, Colleges and Universities. They also have huge homes constructed with marble from floor to ceiling, with a minimum of ten self-contained bedrooms for guests. They move around in bullet proof jeeps and some have fleets of high end cars including Rolls Royce, Bentley, Mercedes, Jaguar and Porsches, to name a few.

They fly first or business class on all flights, especially international flights. Oftentimes, their complete family and personal assistant's luggage alone exceeds the price of a discounted international economy class round trip ticket. They are not concerned with prices. The most insulting treatment they may experience is travel on the French airline that flies from Paris to Abuja in 2018, in an aircraft that does not provide a means to charge electronics during a seven hour international flight. At times, they may require its esteemed Nigerian passengers to board their aircraft by putting their foot on the tarmac, as if boarding air force one, in the rain.

I personally like my hometown airline, Delta Airlines, because it is more accommodating to the Nigeria palate. The rich are well educated. Most attended the best universities in Nigeria, Europe, Canada and America. They reap all the benefits of the privileged elite and they spend money like it grows on trees. What's interesting is, it doesn't matter how much money the rich have or how the wealth was amassed. From the mouth of a Nigerian house boy, "no rich man in Nigeria will ever accept being cheated". The rich or privileged class in Nigeria are adamant about posturing themselves above the fray. Their motto is: Let the truth be told, or as my Quantity Surveyor always says, "Let's call a spade a spade".

The rich and privileged can eliminate people and order people to be eliminated. The rich can lie, cheat and steal and be promoted to higher office (Hum… sounds like another place I know). They can drive their cars any kind of way and they seldom do, but they will provide a dirty slap to their driver if he does so without just cause they can talk to the police and security officials any kind of way. They don't fear the police but they respect the military. The rich don't always respect armed robbers or kidnappers. It is because of pride and lack of respect that many are dealt with harshly, as the rich see them as small boys insulting them.

Moreover, they are often rumored to be the Godfathers to such criminals, as these thugs have neither access to vital information to plan operations, the connection or money to purchase such advanced weapons and vehicles. The rich don't fear power outages because they have two or more high powered diesel generators that run twelve hour shifts, in spite of what the power company provides. They don't fear juju, as they also have their own personal juju person. The rich don't fear the legal system but they acknowledge it.) Nor do they fear health issues because they travel abroad to receive first class treatment. The only thing many of the rich truly fear is *"Poverty"*.

Nigeria, with a population of over 210 million people, has honest and hardworking rich citizens. There are honest Businessmen and Women, Developers, Bankers, Intellectuals, Entertainer's and Movie Moguls. There are also honest Construction Company owners, Athlete's, Hotel and Club owners, Farmers and yes, Lawyers, Judges and Politicians. Many of the rich are too busy making money the old fashioned way, *by Earning it,* and by providing goods and services to an enormous population, that is expected to be the world's third largest by the year 2050. The rich are too busy to be concerned about the dubious distinction created by the corrupt. As previously mentioned, I agree that the distribution of wealth is just one of the key elements of poverty in the country. I must assert, Nigeria, nor the continent of Africa, does not need another temporary hero who will visit and place a bandage on a leak in the Dam.

Who Turned out the Lights?

What Nigerians require is a level playing field for all its citizens, which can be achievable if provided continuous power, good roads (National Transportation System), and an unwavering commitment to a maintenance plan to sustain its infrastructure. Nigeria would attract businesses and professionals ready to establish and create a firm foundation, and facilitate long term employment to the masses. Realizing no developing country can survive without the natural resources provided by the continent of Africa, I assure you there is no progressive minded business CEO anywhere in the world that would not be interested in tapping into the African market. Nigeria is populated with an educated, smart, youthful and enormous population.

Nigeria now embraces Multinational Corporations and smaller businesses such as: Shell Petroleum Development Company Oil & Gas Multinational, Mobil Oil & Gas, Price Waterhouse Cooper (PWC) consulting Multinational, Google Technology Multinational, Halliburton Energy Oil & Gas Multinational, Sheraton Hotels Hospitality Multinational, IBM Technology Multinational, Delta Airlines, McAfee Design & Distributing Co., Inc., KFC, Domino's Pizza, Cold Stone Ice Cream, and Johnny Rockets, just to name a few. The Chinese even have a China Chamber of commerce in the F.C.T. of Abuja.

Who Turned out the Lights?

The enemies to the Republic of Nigeria are everywhere. They come in the form of unequal international trade policies, foreign debt, BoKo haram, corruption, insecurity and poverty. They also come in the form of tribal differences, mismanagement of natural resources, lack of job opportunities for its youth, lack of a good healthcare system, a crumbling infrastructure and out of control crime.

However, if the government would be so humbled to oblige and empower the citizens of its beloved country with, once again, *uninterrupted lights and good roads,* along with an aggressive maintenance plan, this modest but essential action would facilitate such unimaginable progress. Within twenty years, Nigeria would be a second world developing country, with a firm down payment on the first world. Moreover, using the jargon from my hometown city Atlanta, Georgia, Nigeria will also become a country *"too busy to hate."*

 "As long as greed is stronger than compassion, there will always be suffering."

 - Rusty Eric

Who Turned out the Lights?

CHAPTER 11: YOU ARE WELCOME

Today if you are a foreigner visiting Nigeria, you will notice that it is one of the most welcoming countries in the world. You will find that, in spite of the negative propaganda, Nigeria is also a place where normalcy exists and you should have nothing to fear, even though it is considered a third world country.

Nigeria is a place where everyone will greet you good morning and mean it. It's a place where the old are respected and considered wise, and where senior citizens settle more disputes than the police. Nigeria is a place where old men never die, they *just fade away.* Here, many senior citizens live to be 100 years old or older.

Nigeria is a place where the food is mostly organic and plentiful. A place where everyone greets you good morning, good afternoon or good evening before starting a conversation or asking a question. (Here, you can discipline your children so you will see that most children are disciplined. Even the dogs are exceptionally loyal and smart. Nigeria is a place where you may visit and never see a lion, tiger or wild animal, unless you go to the zoo or on a safari there are fine four and five star hotels. Nigeria is a place where marriage is considered a badge of honor. A place where you have high rise buildings in the downtown area of major cities. It's also where Eko Atlantic provides the best prime real estate in West Africa in Nigeria. Not knowing of Fela! Kuti in Lagos is like saying you've never heard of James Brown in Augusta, Georgia USA.

Nigeria is a place where you can fly by commercial airline or private jet from one city to another. You can have money, dignity and respect. You can also use your ATM card to buy fuel for your car and the attendant will pump it. Nigeria is a country that has a democratic government. It is a Country of Laws. The Government will not enact policies to destroy black resolve, and Muslim and Christians live and work in harmony.

Nigeria is a country which welcomes White Americans, German Americans, Russian Americans, Italian Americans, Mexican Americans and especially Black Americans. The police are truly your friend (Police Motto), and there is no police genocide. Nigeria is a country rich in natural resources other than oil. It has colleges and institutions for higher learning in every major city.

Have you ever viewed the movie starring Brad Pitt and Tom Cruise entitled *"Interview with the vampire"?* Louis (Pitt), who was suicidal after the death of his family, was persuaded by Lestat (Cruise) to choose immortality over death. Now, as a vampire, he views the world through his vampire eyes. He sees statues moving, birds talking and clearly in the dark. Similarly, your vision will be clearer after years of visits to Nigeria.

I now see the environment with my Nigerian eyes. I now see the beauty of women carrying their babies meticulously wrapped, sleeping on their backs, with food for sale balanced on their heads while they walk through a busy market place. I also see the strut of the men as they walk majestically, moving slightly to the left or right, to avoid being touched by a vehicle, bike or pedestrian traffic approaching from the front or rear without looking. They utilize their ability to feel their surroundings, (or how) even in an untidy marketplace.

I no longer see the dirt and decay. The delicate and enticing way marketers arrange their goods to attract your eyes to become their customer. At this time, I am at a place where many that have visited will never reach. I now see deeply inside   the country and its people with my Nigerian eyes, and my spirit is calmly whispering to all that I am, saying, *"well-done brother Bilal Mawuli Motilewa"*. ***"You are welcome".***

Who Turned out the Lights?

CHAPTER 12: "DIVINE" PURPOSE

L ife has been good to me. God has blessed me with good health, education and an opportunity to travel much of the world. I have witnessed the worst and the best in people and returned home safely. I've received more awards and positive acknowledgements than most and remain ever grateful to all those who have assisted, embraced and nominated me for honors. I would have never partitioned for such accolades.

No matter the praise or financial gain I have received throughout my life, I have never been settled minded enough to be satisfied. I always harbored an unshakable desire to feel there was always more expected of me, thus I can't really find rest. It is not easy to follow the will of God as the flesh will always be in conflict with the spirit. Thanks to God and prayer, I have learned how to protect my spirit, such that it is always open to receive his voice of reason and wisdom.

For the past nineteen years, when I have been isolated or alone, I cried a river of tears asking my creator why I have such rage in my heart to continue to travel internationally, especially to the country of Nigeria. My mind is often troubled, my wife, family and friends are even concerned and confused. For someone who's first flight was at a young age and   has over a quarter million miles flown, how could I all of a sudden, during the first hours of a twelve hour international flight to Lagos, become paranoid and claustrophobic?

It was like being stuck in a metal tomb or being buried alive. I couldn't get out, it was difficult to catch my breath and I was sweating profusely. I was extremely frightened and I struggled quietly with hundreds of other passengers oblivious to my internal suffering. I remember roaming the isles of the aircraft at thirty six thousand feet above the Atlantic Ocean as if I were a ghost. I was in a struggle for my life but never felt more alive, so the Holy Spirit instructed me to use reason and wisdom.

I prayed and I walked throughout the cabin. I went to the bathroom multiple times, as opening the door to exit gave me a   sense of coming out of a confined space. I drank wine, looked at other passengers, tried to watch movies and ate chocolate. I tried just about everything but nothing seemed to have worked. After several hours battling with anxiety and exhaustion, I fell asleep. I woke up hours later and, reaching the continental tip of Africa, the blinds of the aircraft were opened to reveal a new day. I was met by a warm and direct ray of sunlight from the East, which confirmed that I had survived the night, and *"I thanked God"*.

Who Turned out the Lights?

After twenty-nine days on the ground, I began to be concerned about my return flight home. Could I gather the courage and mental strength to board the plane once more? It was a daunting thought. When the day arrived, I calmly entered the airport with the crew as a Delta Airline medallion member. I often received upgrades and, on this day, I received an upgrade to business class. After checking in, I proceeded to the Delta Airlines VIP section waiting room and noticed a famous African American Reverend. I walked over to greet him as two Americans on foreign soil. We had plenty of time for a lively jovial discussion.

We are both proud graduates of HBCU's. Jokingly he wanted me to know that, as a collegiate football player, he scored so many touchdowns against my school, Florida Agricultural and Mechanical University (FAMU) that our institution made him famous. But, out of respect and realizing his civil rights record and closeness to Dr. Martin Luther King, Jr., I kept my thoughts to myself. I was thinking internally that this brother is about to lose one of the two supporters he had when he contested for the highest political office in America. Prior to boarding, the honorable Reverend was thoughtful enough to say hello to my wife, so I am grateful to the two of them for the calming effect they provided before this flight.

Who Turned out the Lights?

I struggled a bit but was able to protect my thoughts. We arrived safely back to Atlanta twelve hours later. The day was June 8, 2018. I was headed to a meeting in Abuja with my business partner, when I received the dreadful news that my brother and co-owner of our business, Adrian McAfee, passed away. Maybe this was the day I also died. Or was it June 1, 2014, on the crowded streets of Allen Avenue in Ikeja (Lagos), when I got the news that my other brother and company VP Robin ("Bob") passed away?

Maybe it was me the Nigerians were speaking of when they stated that certain people in this eatery are actually dead. Perhaps it was the author who passed away from typhoid or malaria from mosquito bites on Salami Street in Mafoloku. Is it possible with the five systematic deaths within a four-year period, resulting in the loss of the firm's most experienced and loyal business executives, including the death of my beloved Uncle? Maybe the spiritual attack was against our company, and a budding democracy's nefarious forces that was seeking to turn the lights out. (*That is the Spiritual Twine that seemed to bind it all*)

The continent of Africa is a powerfully spiritual place, such that "*whatever is may not be*". However, what I do know is that I've learned how important it is to protect your spirit, and I am truly grateful Allah has provided me with such wisdom. No man actually knows the amount of time humans have existed. It is as far back as the discovery of the skeleton of Lucy 3.2 million years ago, or much-much farther back than that. Based on statistics, our own average American life expectancy is less than 79 years if you are so blessed. Seventy Nine years, in light of the time man has existed feels as if we are strangers, pilgrims on earth, travelers just passing through. It's just as if it's only a moment in time… it's truly short.

I believe what truly matters is what you and I do with that moment given to us. Did we try to follow God's instructions for our lives, in that moment? Did we try to love our neighbors as we loved ourselves, in that moment? Did we try to show compassion to all God's children, in that moment? Those questions can only be answered by you. When my time is up I hope it will be said that "I really tried".

It would be presumptuous of me to think I am someone so anointed with the responsibility to bring about a renewed psychological reconnection between Africans and Black Americans. Would it be overly bold of me to think that, as a Black American Construction Company CEO, our success could be the spark that ignites a new wave of confidence between Black American professionals and businesses, causing them to no longer fear Africa? Would it be presumptuous to believe that the souls of those 12.5 million of the brightest minds and most able bodies, who were kidnapped from the continent to the Americas, are crying out like a tree falling in the forest, with only a select few empowered with the *" Divine Purpose"* to heed their calls.

As CEO, despite the many battles, victories or moments of defeat, we never wavered in our determination to seek a peaceful resolution and move forward without carrying animosity. As Businessmen, we understood that no matter the depth of the unfair treatment committed against us, we must be mindful of the faults committed on our part. Similarly, African history should not allow us to forget the actions of African fighters in the Benin Expedition, the Rwandan genocide against the Tutsi between April and June 1994, resulting in the slaughter of an estimated 800,000 Rwandans.

We should not forget the NATO exercise in 2011 against Libya, which may exemplify three examples of brutalities carried out by Africans against other Africans. Additionally, Black Americans today have a spending capacity of over one Trillion dollars, which would make us the 9th wealthiest nation in the world. It's the lack of economic unity that creates disrespect, therefore, our mothers weep daily for the brutal treatment of its children. We ask, is it possibly the reason that black descendant's children's teeth are now on edge? I have the present conviction to seek forgiveness, first for my own shortcomings, and those committed by our fathers before casting stones at others.

The continent of **Africa** does not need to censure anyone for its present condition. **No one can come to Africa and save it but Africans** As McAfee Design & Distributing Co. Inc.'s late superintendent, "Dad", would say during a time requiring a sense of urgency, "we *call on every good man to get into the hole"*. From the hole the work shall begin. You will feel the warmth of **the sun,** but you can't claim its impressive radiance. From the depths of the hole you must build a modern and **firm foundation** by stepping up your game. As you work, be so bold not to worry about the haters standing above on the sidelines watching, and planning your demise. But know you have the strength of spirit to receive instruction from Allah, because all historical evidence reveals that the land of your fathers is the birthplace of humanity.

The negative propaganda nor the **dubious distinction** casted upon the people will not stifle your mission. Remain steadfast with the moral **courage to hope (,)** as you build with Muslims, Christians, **the rich** and indigent. With the ancestral power from the **Ancient**

Who Turned out the Lights?

City of Benin, and knowledge of Timbuktu from your glorious past unified, you will toil hand in hand until you find common ground. **The sun** will provide the way forward. Through this abiding unity the country will advance and the world will bear-witness to the true *Giant of Africa,* and together the children of men shall reach for the light. *

Author Goodwill Ambassador Alfonso McAfee, Jr.

30 August 2019   Benin City Edo State Nigeria

GLOSSARY

ATM – Automated Teller machine

Area Boys-(Also known as Agberos) Loosely organized gangs of street children and teenagers, composed mostly of men who roam the streets of Lagos in Lagos State Nigeria.

Beam me up Scotty- A catchphrase that made its way into popular culture from the science fiction television series Star Trek. It comes from the command that Captain Kirk gives Chief engineer Montgomery "Scotty" Scott when he needs to be transported back to Starship Enterprise.

Binis A cultural group living in or around Benin City in Nigeria.

Bookworms- An individual who loves and frequently reads books, although bookworm is sometimes used pejoratively.

Boot- The luggage space in a vehicle or the trunk of a car.

Brits- A British person.

Budding engineer- Recent engineering graduate with limited work experience, in training.

Who Turned out the Lights?

Caveat- A warning or provision of specific stipulations, conditions or limitations.

Civets- Six favorite emerging market countries: Columbia, Vietnam, Egypt, South Korea, Iran and Indonesia.

Chill out- To become calmer; Slang for relax

Come down- Means it's getting serious or real get out of your vehicle.

Coup E'tat- Forced overthrow of current leadership from
within

DPO- Divisional Police Officer or Data Protection Officer

Eze- An Igbo word which means king.

FAMU- Florida Agricultural and Mechanical University located in Tallahassee, Florida USA

FCT- Federal Capital Territory in Nigeria

FELA KUTI – Fela Anikulapo Kuti, also professionally Known as Fela Kuti, was a Nigerian multi-instrumentalist, musician, composer and pioneer of the Afro beat music genre and human rights activist.

FG – Federal Government

Who Turned out the Lights?

FMCG – Fast-moving consumer goods

FUFU – Dough made from boiled and ground plantain or cassava, used as a staple food in parts of West and Central Africa.

GDP – Gross Domestic Product

Genteel – Characterized by exaggerated or affected politeness, refinement or respectability.

Ghana must go bag – A popular name given to the migration of several West African citizens. A type of cheap matted woven nylon zipped tote bag used by the migrants to move their belongings.

Going Postal – An American English slang phrase referring to becoming extremely and uncontrollably angry, often to the point of violence, and usually in a workplace environment.

HBCU – Historically Black College and University

Hinterland – The remote areas of a country away from the coast or the banks of major rivers.

Immemorial – Originating in the distant past, very old.

Inimical – Tending to obstruct or harm.

Iron Lady – A nickname used to describe female heads of government around the world; "Strong willed" women.

Who Turned out the Lights?

James Joseph Brown – An American singer, writer, dancer, musician, record producer and band leader. A progenitor of funk music and a major figure of 20th century music and dance. He is often referred to as the "Godfather of Soul".

KFC – Kentucky Fried Chicken

LGBT –Lesbian, Gay, Bi-sexual and Transgender

Michigan Lottery – A legal game of chance, which offers numerous online and scratch off games, giving players a wide variety of prize possibilities.

Motherland – The country in which you or your ancestors were born and to which you still feel emotionally linked, even if you live somewhere else.

NAF – Nigerian Air Force

Nefarious – Wicked or criminal (typical of an action or activity)

Next Tomorrow- Nigerian slang for the day after tomorrow.

NYC - The city of New York, usually called New York City or (NYC) is the most populous city in the United States.

NEPA – National Electric Power Authority

Who Turned out the Lights?

Okada A motorcycle taxi. The name was borrowed for Okada Air, a Nigerian local airline, now defunct.

Oga – A Yoruba word, so you may regard this post as a short course in Yoruba language. Oga means "master" or "the boss" or "leader". An Oga is the top man or women and this usually carries some form of power. An Oga is a powerful person.

OILG – Refers to Oshodi-Isolo Local Government area within the city of Lagos Nigeria.

Particulars – All necessary documents required to legally operate a vehicle in Nigeria, original or copies should always be carried in the vehicle and presented to police upon request.

Quagmire – A situation that is so difficult or complicated that you cannot make much progress.

Revenant – A noun meaning, "One who has returned, as if from the dead."

ROR – Robinson O Robinson

Sachet water – Began in 1990. It is a sustainable clean, safe drinking water packaging. It is a relatively new and fast growing source of drinking water worldwide Popularly referred to as "pure water' sachets have gained public affinity due to the low price, convenience, ubiquity, and the public perception that sachet water is of higher quality and safer than tap water.

Second – In Nigeria it often means your first assistance or a person very close to you.

Somehow like that – In Nigeria it means a way to describe someone or something usually another person.

Strapped up – In construction it means to put on your tool belt and other work related gear.

VIP – Very Important Person

VI – Victoria Island, a more upscale section in Lagos Nigeria

4-1-9 – An Advance-fee scam is a form of fraud and is one of the most common types of confidence tricks… The number "4-1-9" refers to the section of the Nigerian Criminal code dealing with fraud, the charges and penalties for offenders.

ABOUT THE AUTHOR

Alfonso McAfee Jr., Goodwill Ambassador and Chief Executive Officer (CEO) of McAfee Design & Distributing Co., Inc. headquartered in Atlanta Georgia.

Mr. McAfee earned the MBEP from the private Ivy League Dartmouth College, Tuck School of Business. He also received a BS in Civil Engineering from The Florida A&M University. McAfee Design is the recipient of the National Minority Construction Firm of the year awarded by the US Department of Commerce.

Mr. McAfee was featured on the cover of the Atlanta Tribune Magazine as Trailblazer of the year for Construction. McAfee Design has completed 3 major construction projects in Nigeria along with a plethora of international and domestic projects. Mr. McAfee shares his unique perspective on Nigeria's people, culture and traditions.